LOVE
LIKE
FIRE

CASSANDRA SOARS

CHARISMA
HOUSE

LOVE LIKE FIRE by Cassandra Soars
Published by Charisma House
Charisma Media/Charisma House Book Group
600 Rinehart Road
Lake Mary, Florida 32746
www.charismahouse.com

Cover design by: Lisa Rae McClure
Design Director: Justin Evans

Visit the author's website at cassandrasoars.com.

Library of Congress Cataloging-in-Publication Data:
Names: Soars, Cassandra, author.
Title: Love like fire / Cassandra Soars.
Description: First edition. | Lake Mary : Charisma House, 2016. | Includes
   bibliographical references and index.
Identifiers: LCCN 2015051235 (print) | LCCN 2016005705 (ebook)

I endorse Cassandra Soars with great love. I am grateful for the ways Cassandra poured out her life in Pemba. Her book, *Love Like Fire*, captures the joys and challenges of life on the mission field. It describes one of the hardest seasons in my life, but God is faithful and has restored all things beyond what I could have imagined, miraculously healing Rolland. I pray that each person who reads this will be encouraged to allow God to take hold of their lives and give everything for His glory, even in the toughest circumstances.

—HEIDI G. BAKER, PHD
COFOUNDER AND DIRECTOR OF IRIS GLOBAL

As I read Cassandra Soars's book *Love Like Fire*—about Heidi Baker and her life—I felt pulled along in God's river of liquid love and fire. What a unique and totally yielded life and ministry and what an example to follow. I highly recommend this book to everyone.

—REINHARD BONNKE
FOUNDER, CHRIST FOR ALL NATIONS

Heidi Baker is one of my favorite "heroes/sheroes." I have known her both in public ministry and in private sessions, and I can truthfully say she is one of the most authentic people I know. She is living, walking *love* and has truly been an inspiration to me. *Love Like Fire* will move you emotionally and will invite you through passion to a walk of selfless love—the highest calling in the kingdom. I cherish this book; it reveals the heart of God. I cherish this book…and I cherish Heidi.

—PATRICIA KING
FOUNDER, XP MINISTRIES

Heidi Baker is the most amazing Christian I know. Her story is one of love, compassion, and supernatural power. Her story is amazing, making good material for an amazing book. I am glad we have a book not just about part of Heidi's life, but about her life. If you enjoy love stories, you will love this book. If you love adventure stories, you will love this book. If you love stories of sacrificial love, you will love this book. If you love stories about supernatural miracles, you will love this book. If you love stories of supernatural provision, you will love this book. *Love Like Fire* is a must-read for all.

—RANDY CLARK, DMIN
FOUNDER AND PRESIDENT, GLOBAL AWAKENING

Legends are often grounded in truth. And though the stories in this book have that legendary quality we so often read about in the stories of saints of old, I can assure you that the stories in this book are not embellished. They are all true. I have never met a person so abandoned to God as Heidi Baker. I have personally observed her in the midst of precarious situations, such as calming people down during violent riots, boldly preaching to witch doctors holding venomous snakes, and cradling dying children in her arms. In every situation, she is fearless. The Bible says there is no fear in love. Heidi is truly in love, first of all with Jesus, and then with the least, the last, the lost, and the broken. *Love Like Fire* will surely inspire you to love others more deeply as well.

—STACEY CAMPBELL
COFOUNDER, BE A HERO (BEAHEROINTERNATIONAL.ORG)

My wife, Barbara, and I met Heidi Baker in the fall of 2000. I first saw her lying prostrate on a dirt floor in a Nigerian church. Her demeanor was essentially self-effacing, and I only learned about her depth a few years later. She challenged me then and she challenges me now. As famous as she is, the light shining *on* her is not brighter than the light shining *in* her, and an unobservant person will fail to see it.

Cassandra Soars began attending our church as a student, and I soon recognized in her a passion for the pursuit of God. I can think of no better combination of author and personality to produce a story, which will powerfully change the hearts of a multitude. As I read this book, I wanted to get saved all over again!

—BISHOP JOSEPH L. GARLINGTON, SR.
SENIOR PASTOR, COVENANT CHURCH OF PITTSBURGH
PRESIDING BISHOP, RECONCILIATION! AN INTERNATIONAL
NETWORK OF CHURCHES AND MINISTRIES

Few people on earth have the capacity and the zeal to love like Heidi Baker. She loves like unquenchable fire. Her poured-out life has transformed Mozambique, southern Africa, and indeed the entire world. Cassandra Soars has done an amazing job in capturing Heidi Baker's incredible story.

—JOHN ARNOTT
COFOUNDER, CATCH THE FIRE
OVERSEER, PARTNERS IN HARVEST

I have known Rolland and Heidi Baker for many years now and count their friendship as an honor. Their love for Jesus is wonderfully displayed in all of the countries they minister in. I have seen firsthand the results of the message they bring and its miraculous results. I encourage you to read this account of their life and love for God, and in turn that you let it transform your life.

—DAVID L. HOGAN
MISSIONARY TO MEXICO
FOUNDER OF FREEDOM MINISTRIES

It is impossible to spend time with Heidi Baker and not be impacted by the intense and divine love that drips from her words and shines from her eyes. Reading *Love Like Fire* was like spending a few days with Heidi, hearing her stories and seeing her in action. *Love Like Fire* has captured the essence, the value system, the unreasonable perseverance, and the boundless love that energizes and compels Heidi. If you've never met Heidi, you will meet her in the pages of this book. More than that, you will be confronted with the burning and relentless love of God that transforms everything it touches. Your life, your plans, and the world around you may never be the same!

—CHARLES STOCK
SENIOR PASTOR, LIFE CENTER, HARRISBURG, PENNSYLVANIA

The moment I picked up *Love like Fire*, I could not put it down. It has captured the story of Heidi Baker, sharing a simple young girl's adventure into the miraculous. From Heidi's early years growing up in Southern California to her life today leading a global missions organization that touches the world, this book unpacks Heidi's story with depth and detail that will inspire the reader to live a life of love and sacrifice. I encourage you to read this book and let Heidi's story change your life.

—Dennis Flom

Iris Global, Redding, California

I have read many books in my life and very seldom does a book captivate me the way this one did. I could not put it down. Cassandra Soars has a way of carrying you into the story. Her ability to draw you into Heidi Baker's journey is so real that with every word you partake of her life experiences. You will not just read this book; you will live it. As I read each chapter I "met" the people, "saw" the places, cried with each of them, and rejoiced in their triumphs. This book caused my faith to increase tremendously and challenged me to love and pursue God with intense passion.

This book will inspire you and will change you. It will take you into higher heavenly realms and will cause you to live an extraordinary life as you walk among real and ordinary people like Jesus did!

—Isabel Allum

Cofounder, Forest City Destiny Church
in London, Ontario

Heidi Baker is one of God's warriors and heroes on the front lines of the spiritual battles in Africa today. The story of Mozambique will live on for generations. Read the struggles, the victories, and the forward motion of the kingdom of God in this story about the ministry of the Holy Spirit through Heidi. She is a friend; we're coworkers in Christ. Iris and YWAM partner together in many parts of the world. Read, enjoy, and put into practice the principles Heidi has used in serving the Lord and you too will have been inspired, thrilled, informed, and motivated to fulfill your destiny here on earth.

—Loren Cunningham

Founder, Youth With a Mission

| ISBN
  9781629986784 (trade paper : alk. paper) | ISBN 9781629986791
(e-book)
Subjects: LCSH: Baker, Heidi, 1959- | Baker, Rolland. |
  Missionaries--Mozambique--Biography.
Classification: LCC BV3625.M65 S63 2016 (print) | LCC BV3625.
M65 (ebook) |
  DDC 266.0092/2679--dc23
LC record available at http://lccn.loc.gov/2015051235

All accounts of miraculous healing or supernatural events were either witnessed by the author or by Heidi Baker.

Some names and identifying details have been changed to protect the privacy of individuals.

First edition

16 17 18 19 20 — 987654321
Printed in the United States of America

CONTENTS

PART IV
STOPPING FOR THE ONE

PART V
COMING BACK

INTRODUCTION

THIS IS A story about the people who taught me the most about how to love.

When I was a small girl, I used to lay awake at night and think about the ways I could make the world better. My ten-year-old heart was old, and it especially ached for those who were hurting. Somewhere I had heard about "poor people" on the other side of the world, no matter that we were poor on this side of the world—I'm not sure I knew that. I dreamed that someday I would be rich and own private planes to bring the poor to America where they could live in large buildings I owned. Childish dreams.

When I was a junior in college, I heard Heidi Baker speak at a conference. The passion for the Y-shaped country of Mozambique and the vulnerable children of the burnt-orange land was evident in her voice. Her stories reminded me of my childhood dreams to provide a better life for those suffering.

At the same time I couldn't help but wonder why she would give up everything to live in one of the poorest countries in the world. A comfortable life in "Amer-i-ca," was one that most of the Mozambicans would want. They pronounced it as if it were the place that embodied all their dreams, the land that promised *alegria* (happiness). Heidi was obviously happy in Mozambique.

Heidi spoke of her adopted children, their lives on the streets before she found them—the girls who had been raped, the boys who had been molested and the ones who had molested others or who had been commissioned to steal, the people who lived in the garbage dump—and the way their lives changed after she adopted them. Her stories were heartrending, and it almost hurt to listen to them. The people attending the conference treated her with the utmost admiration, waiting around in large groups to talk to her. All were eager for a word or a blessing or a hug, treating her like a saint, like one of her own heroes, Mother Teresa.

The day after she spoke at that conference, Heidi Baker was on a plane back to what I thought must be a sorrow-filled country where she found joy. I was back to my daily routine in college, and her beautiful land and children seemed very far away.

When I graduated, I found myself in a place not so different from the impoverished conditions Heidi Baker described—not enough resources to teach children who were for all intents orphans (their mothers crack-addicts and their fathers missing or unknown).

The school in the inner city of Pittsburgh where I taught high school English was dilapidated to say the least, and I was embarrassed for the man who took me on a tour of the small school. His eyes and tone were apologetic, and when he showed me the lunchroom in the basement, I felt a bit suffocated—the same way I felt while working at the residential treatment facility, a place for kids who either didn't have parents or whose parents weren't equipped to care for them for one reason or another. I left because I couldn't stand to see the workers abuse the children, who had suffered enough abuse in their short lives. As the surroundings of the dingy school closed in around me, I wondered if this would be a place where I could make a difference, and I shrugged off the feeling I got from the cold, unfinished basement.

In the classroom where I taught, I pretended to be more stern than I was as the teenagers sat at their desks. Their problems were so big: one of my students wrote about being sexually abused and being born as a result of incest. Her father was also her grandfather, who had raped her mother. Another student's mother died and he was left an orphan who molested his younger cousins when his aunt took him in. I wanted so badly to help them and see them succeed, but it felt like they had a difficult time imagining life to be any different.

Success often meant leaving their neighborhoods, friends, and family, as well as the familiarity, which was all the security they had ever known. I gave them what I could, all the education and love and care they were willing to receive, but due to a lack of resources, the high school closed down the following year. So I left the inner city to pursue a graduate degree in writing. Academia was a far cry from the life of the inner city, where grown men rocked back and forth on street corners and whistled at me when I walked by.

Identity politics was the discourse of the academy, and everyone seemed to be interested in social justice, but very few actually knew how to do anything practical to relieve suffering. They could talk well, but not much came from their theorizing. They were Foucault's intellectuals: ones who seemed incapable of action. They did, however, raise the question: What gives someone the right to intervene in the lives of others? It was the main critique of imperialism and colonialism. Some said all development and humanitarian intervention was imperialist. But that argument was too easy because it excused them from doing anything to help those who were suffering.

I finished graduate school and began teaching college

writing and composition classes. I wrote the curriculum and centered my composition classes on the theme of social change. What better way for freshmen students to learn to think analytically than to grapple with concepts of social justice and extreme poverty? While my students became more sensitive and globally aware, I started reading about the continent of Africa and the complexities of its issues. When I read about the Scramble for Africa, when European leaders in the late 1800s and early 1900s carved up the continent for themselves, I felt sad and angry at the injustice.

I longed to do more, and I realized that writing about Africa was one way to do something. I thought back to Heidi Baker and Mozambique. It was one of the poorest countries in the world, a country recovering from floods, drought, and a civil war. I would start there and find my story along the way through a process called immersion journalism.

I told the university I was going to Africa to do research for a book and that I wouldn't be available to teach for the spring semester but planned on returning for the fall. I left for Pemba, Mozambique, a remote northern rural town on the coast, where Heidi and her husband Rolland were based. My plan was to return to the university after a semester away to continue building a career as a college professor in the English department. I was wrong about the four months. I ended up staying in Mozambique for the good part of seven years. The project itself became something much larger.

I did not know at the time that I would relocate to one of the poorest countries in the world, nor did I know that I was about to embark on another type of education, one that would become the foundation for the rest of my life. I did not expect all the changes that would result from the decision to write about Africa. Nor did I expect to learn a new way of living. Heidi exemplified living in the Spirit, a way of life tinged with the supernatural the way fire consumed the burnt offerings in the Old Testament, the Spirit's fire consuming fallen human nature as flesh and bones surrendered to something higher than its own material comfort, something far better than the American dream. At first, as I observed Heidi's way of life, I struggled to comprehend it. In the process of observing and interviewing and living alongside Heidi and her work, I unexpectedly moved from observer to participant, and Heidi became a spiritual mother to me.

I was in Mozambique to study Africa, and I wanted to write something that would move people on behalf of the poor. In terms of social justice and taking action, writing was my main way to contribute.

As I encountered extreme poverty for the first time, I understood that I had much to learn before I could ever hope to write (or do) something helpful. The issues were too complex. After almost a year in Mozambique I decided to complete a postgraduate degree in international development at the University of London's School of Oriental and African Studies, which would help me understand the interplay of economics, history, poverty, corruption, and the role of government. It was a one-year Master's degree, and when I finished the course work nine months later, I returned to Mozambique to do research for my dissertation. It was then that I met my husband, Steve.

When Steve and I married, almost three years after I went to Mozambique the first time, we decided to permanently move to Mozambique together and become part of the full-time team of Iris Global, where we developed a vocational training program for the teenagers and then also took on administrative roles in the ministry. A few years later I fell into the role of Heidi's assistant because I had the skill set she needed when she was in serious need of help. This is the reason I have such an insider's view near the end of the book. Because this story is about Heidi, I tried my best to stay out of it and only give necessary contextual information about me as the narrator.

Now, ten years after moving to Africa to do research for a book I hoped to write to raise awareness about extreme poverty, I realize that at some point along the way I moved from objective observer to family. The book I intended to write, the one you are now holding in your hands, is not about the issues plaguing Africa. It is about the issues plaguing humanity and one ministry—one woman—willing to do something about them.

Suffering still is (and probably will always be) occurring on a major scale. After the mass destruction of the Holocaust and World War II, the world said, "Never again." But we sat by during the genocide in Rwanda of almost one million people, and we are often still sitting.

Heidi was different. She spoke of stopping for the one. Not hundreds of thousands, but one. One life—the one in front of you. Imagine if everyone stopped for just one. And then one more. And then maybe another one.

In these pages you will find stories of faith and healing that have been experienced as tangibly as one experiences the heat of the tropical sun or a warm embrace. These stories are not dogmatic or dead, and best of all they are not a figment of someone's hopeful imagination.

While this is ultimately Heidi's story, it's also a story of the impact she has had on others, myself included. As mothers so often shape their daughters, she has helped shape me into a better lover of people. In my thirty-some years I haven't met anyone who loves better than she or anyone else whose love personally impacts hundreds of thousands of people the world over.

It's been said that the greatest type of love is self-sacrificial. Jesus Himself said, "Greater love has no man than this: that a man lay down his life for his friends."[1] Heidi has learned how to love even when it hurts. This is her story and the story of a love that spreads like fire.

Part I

Mama Aida

Chapter 1

CHRISTMAS IN MOZAMBIQUE

S TANDING OUTSIDE THE small airport in Pemba, Mozambique, a country on the southeast coast of Africa, I squinted in the brightest sunlight I had ever seen. The humidity of the one-hundred-plus-degree weather made my clothes stick to my skin. It was December 2005, and though it was just weeks before Christmas, there was nothing that even slightly resembled Christmas. I left the music, decorations, and Christmas trees far behind in the gargantuan European airports that dwarfed this tiny two-story building. As I looked around while waiting for someone to pick me up, I became self-conscious of my pale skin. I realized I would learn what it felt like to be a minority.

After I had been sitting for almost an hour in the sweltering heat, two women arrived in a truck with a closed cab that held two metal benches. Eight little boys crowded the seats, leaving barely enough room for the two enormous pieces of luggage in which I'd packed all the things I thought I would possibly need in Africa.

I squeezed in next to the boys and tried hard not to be intimidated as they stared openly at me. They chattered in Portuguese, a language I didn't yet know. The boys, between eight and ten years old, were from Iris Ministries (now Iris Global), an organization founded by Heidi and Rolland Baker and headquartered in Pemba, Mozambique, where the Bakers cared for two hundred vulnerable children.

The children all called Heidi "Mama Aida," which was Portuguese for "Mama Heidi." At the time I arrived in Mozambique, Heidi and Rolland Baker's multi-country ministry cared for at least a thousand children in Mozambique and thousands more around the world. A few years later they would care for more than six thousand children, and a few years after that the number would balloon to ten thousand. Heidi's vision for Iris was to care for a million children in her lifetime.

I smiled at the boys and glanced out at the landscape, noticing the warm light reflecting off of hard surfaces, the openness of the people's faces, the raw natural beauty of the place, and the poverty (oh my, the poverty!), with ripped holes in clothing so big that shirts barely hung on to skinny frames. I had no reference for this type of poverty; I had experienced the relative poverty of living below the national average income but never the back-breaking poverty of hunger.

On the way to the base I was struck by the stunning blues and greens of the Indian Ocean. No one had told me the children's center was just across the street from the sea. The coastline was unspoiled, and the black-and-white sand glittered in the light of the setting sun over the turquoise water, the beauty contrasting sharply against the poverty. I had tried to prepare myself for the poverty, but I was not prepared for all the beauty and love I found in Africa, a region so typically characterized by war, famine, and disease.

When I arrived at the children's center, the kids gathered around me, played with my hair, and tugged on my hand, and after I sat down, one of them fell asleep on my lap. Though she smelled like urine, I was aware of this small girl's vulnerability, and rather than reject her because she smelled, I let her relax into my arms, her arms loosely around me in a posture of trust.

I got lost my first night in Mozambique. I didn't know how to find my way to my room. The missionary who gave me a tour dropped me off near the front gate where she lived, leaving me suddenly alone. Though I was a professional woman in my mid-twenties, I felt like a child longing for the familiarity of home while standing in the dark under a massive baobab tree.

I walked toward the place I thought might be my building, a one-room concrete hut with a tin roof. When I discovered nothing but a noisy generator where I thought my hut would be, I knew I would not find my way back without asking for help. Waiting for someone to pass me on the dirt path, I stood there next to the humming generator, trying to remember what the path had looked like during the day. I could only remember a tall bamboo fence. When a volunteer, an American girl about my age, walked toward me, I was relieved that I was able to ask her in English if she knew where I was staying. She pointed to my left and said, "Follow that road to the end and make a right, and your house will be in front of you." She was slightly abrupt, but I was grateful for the directions.

I could see my hut from a distance, the harsh shade of blue paint just visible in the moonlight. When I arrived, I opened the heavy wooden door that scraped the concrete floor and walked inside. I flipped the light switch, but I remained in darkness, wondering if there was ever electricity. I rummaged around in my suitcase for what seemed like thirty minutes. I had packed so many random things, and because they were all vacuum-packed in airtight bags, I could not find a single thing I needed, not even a flashlight.

The communal bathroom I shared with four or five other people was across from my hut, and as I made my way there in the dark, I prayed there would be no snakes, spiders, or cockroaches. I could see that there was a toilet, sink, and shower, but I wondered how they worked since there was no running water. I was really wishing I had been able to shower or at least wash the dirt off my face before I fell into bed.

It had been almost 120 degrees before the sun went down at 6:00 p.m. I tried once more to find a flashlight, but I couldn't even find clothes suitable to sleep in. Slightly shaken, I climbed under the mosquito net and lay down in very dirty clothes, and as I did, I briefly remembered the four-year-old child who had fallen asleep in my lap earlier that day; she had smelled of urine and sweat, and I thought about how I probably smelled the same. I had only a piece of toilet paper from the bathroom to continually wipe away the sweat that trickled down my face and neck.

I fell asleep wondering what I had gotten myself into and briefly thought of the absolute trust and rest of the small child and longed to feel the same.

The next morning I awoke at 4:00 a.m. and the sun was shining through the windows, which were holes in the concrete walls covered with screens. I heard the sounds of people talking, babies crying, and a rooster crowing, the sound so close it seemed the rooster was on the roof. Though it was only 4:00 a.m., the sun was bright, and I knew if I didn't get up to explore immediately, I would only become more timid as I thought about all the things I needed to learn just to meet my basic needs.

I opened my door to a Mozambican woman sitting just outside. In a mixture of charades and sign language I asked her how to flush the toilet. She kindly showed me the small bucket floating on top of a large bucket of water. She scooped it full and poured it down into the toilet bowl. The woman, the wife of a respected Mozambican pastor who had been in the army and fought in the civil war, was motherly and kind.

I learned her name was Juliana, and then she mimicked how to take a bucket shower by using the same small bucket to pour over her head while standing over the drain. Later I found out that some visitors had not known this and had bathed in the large buckets of water, plopping their bodies right down into the entire supply of clean water. I could understand how they assumed that is what the water was for, because the bucket was almost waist high.

I wanted to ask her all of my questions, but the language barrier made it difficult to communicate in-depth.

In traditional Mozambican society women typically take care of the home. Juliana stayed in her house doing the laundry, household chores, and cooking while her husband, Pastor Guillermo, a respected member of the community, attended to his duties as a church leader.

A few months after my arrival, however, the community was shocked when Heidi asked Pastor Guillermo to step down from his position. It was obvious then why Juliana had a black eye; she could no longer hide the effects of his beating. Beating a woman was sometimes acceptable in the traditional Mozambican culture, though not in the international Iris culture. Pastor Guillermo, who was no longer supposed to be called "Pastor," became demoralized. You could see it in his downcast eyes. A few months later he died. His young son would continue to live at the children's center and Juliana became a *tia* (auntie), which is what they called the Mozambican women who lived with the children and attended to their daily needs.

My first morning in Pemba, after Juliana's help, I found my way across the street to the beach where I sat under a palm tree overlooking fishermen preparing their brightly painted canoes for the day's work. It was noisy from the crowds of barefoot women who were chattering and shouting greetings to one another as they walked behind me on the road. They wore beautifully dyed fabric. I tried to focus on the bright colors of the sea in front of me instead of the unfamiliar feelings of fear and uncertainty.

The shock of something so new and foreign—full immersion into a different culture—made me feel like a child again, only I was aware that I knew absolutely nothing in a way children are not. I reminded myself that I needed to experience this in order to write effectively about poverty and cultural differences to Western readers. This thought gave me comfort in this unfamiliar place. If I had already known Heidi's story, I probably would have wondered what she experienced thirty-some years earlier when she first moved from Laguna Beach to the slums of the third world. But I hadn't heard her story yet.

A week later Heidi invited me to dinner with her, Rolland, some of the new volunteers to Iris, and fifteen of the children. She heard from one of her staff that I would be living at the base and volunteering while I conducted research for a book. She was the last to arrive at the ocean-front patio area of the restaurant where we were all mingling. She made sure she greeted each person, spending extra time with the ones who stood awkwardly to the side to make them feel at ease.

Heidi moved as gracefully as a dancer through the crowd. Her posture was that of a ballerina; when stationary in conversation she seemed unaware that she naturally posed in ballet's fourth position. Heidi knelt to talk to each child, listening to their stories and hugging them close before they ran away smiling and shouting to their friends. After connecting with each one, she sat down to a plate of food that had already grown cold. She didn't seem to mind.

The children had finished eating by then, and some of the young girls, who were on the traditional African dance team, practiced their dances by the water. They giggled and talked enthusiastically as they danced, their braids swinging through the air.

"Look at those faces," Heidi said smiling, obviously delighted. "No pictures for sad TV commercials there; we don't have those except when they first come to us." Her face was smooth even when she laughed. Heidi was a petite woman at five feet, four inches, with bright blue eyes, short blonde hair neatly swept to the side, and a heart-shaped face. She looked sophisticated without trying.

Heidi didn't fit the stereotype of a missionary working in sub-standard conditions in the third world. Her tailored black dress, Prada sunglasses, and designer handbag (full to over-flowing with things), and the way she gingerly placed the linen napkin on her lap before eating were all indicators that she enjoyed fine things. While she could have easily been out to dinner at one of Los Angeles' finest restaurants, she was in Mozambique spending Christmas in soaring tropical temper-atures and eating cold chicken.

Heidi's husband, Rolland, was more introverted than she was. He was slender and tall and wore glasses that gave him an air of intellectualism that suited his dry but sometimes giddy humor. I first met him when he casually strolled over and made a sarcastic quip as if we had known each other for years. As it sometimes is with brilliant people, Rolland seemed most comfortable communicating with wit and dry humor.

In contrast, Heidi seemed absolutely earnest and extremely passionate about their work. As she told me about her arrival in Mozambique, she spoke with an easy and innocent tone and seemed childlike. Like me, she had arrived in Africa alone and without a plan. Not knowing anyone, she spent her days sitting on the street corners, getting to know the street children. Then she began to learn their language—both Portuguese and Shangaana, their African dialect.

On her first visit to the government-run children's center in Maputo, she noticed machine gun holes in the walls and rats clambering out of open pipes. The concrete, Portuguese-style buildings had once been aesthetically pleasing with their arches and precise square shapes, but because of the war they were now in shambles. Some of the roofs were caving in. Goats were kept in some of the rooms, and it was hard to tell which rooms were for the animals and which were for the children. The place reeked of feces. She contemplated actually plugging her nose.

Heidi almost wept when she saw the state the children were in. Once a day the kids ate a sort of thin gruel made out of cornmeal. Their bellies were bloated, and they all had worms in their feet because none had any shoes. They wore blank stares on their faces and slept on the concrete floor. Almost no one in Mozambique owned pillows or mattresses, let alone sheets. Heidi had never seen worse conditions.

The picture she painted for me was quite a contrast to the beautiful kids with the shining faces who sat across from us at dinner that night. As she talked, Heidi became more and more energized, while I became more and more fascinated with her story. The Bakers started with absolutely nothing— no money, no contacts in the country, no staff—and it was obvious that what they had accomplished was extraordinary. I could sense Rolland and Heidi's passion when they told me how they were now feeding thirteen thousand people a day (which rose to one hundred thousand when the next floods struck).

All over Mozambique and Malawi thousands of churches

had been started and thousands of vulnerable children were being fed, clothed, and loved. Various medical clinics, Bible colleges, small businesses, and construction projects had sprung up in every direction. Iris was also doing work in nearly thirty other countries, including Sudan, Brazil, and India. I knew the list could continue, and the number of children they were taking in grew by the day.

Heidi said her motivation was love. "We are trying to do one thing: we are trying to learn how to love," she said. "This is our job. It's our only goal. We are not a slick bunch, but we are trying to learn how to love. This is what our work is about. It's about incarnational love, and love looks like something. To a mother whose child is dying from malaria, it looks like malaria medication."

"I don't want anyone classifying us as a humanitarian organization," Rolland added after Heidi finished telling me about the various kinds of work Iris was doing.

"What do you want to be classified as?" I asked.

"A revival," he said. "Out of control, moving like fire across Africa."

"The gospel is comprehensive and includes healing for every part—spiritual as well as physical—and that's what we're interested in too," Rolland continued. "There are two camps in the world—those who believe it, and those who don't, who run around trying to fix the world and don't get very far or see lasting results."

Christians tend to ask why they do humanitarian work and don't solely focus on the spiritual needs of the people, Rolland said with some disdain, implying that the answer was obvious: love is holistic.

Rolland looked off into the distance as he talked, his mind completely focused on whatever topic he was discussing at the moment. It seemed he was oblivious to the noise and distractions around us. Children ran past him, shouting, "Papa Rolland, Papa Rolland!" He glanced briefly at them, said, "Hi," expressionlessly, and kept talking without losing his train of thought.

Rolland continued, "I couldn't imagine myself doing this kind of work, but it turned out to be more critical and important than anything I could be doing."

As I listened to their story, I became more intrigued. They knew I was there for research, yet they spent almost the entire meal initiating conversation and sharing their story with me.

I learned later that Rolland was the administrative genius in the background of the ministry, playing a crucial role. Behind the scenes he took care of the myriad details that come with running an international organization in a third-world country. When I asked him why his work was more important than anything, he answered thoroughly, as he often does, addressing the question from every angle.

"The best part is bringing love where there wasn't any and that spilling over into the most impossible situations. It accomplishes something nothing else can. There is a whole class of very successful rich people in their fifties and sixties, but inside they're like lost children, asking, 'What are we going to do with our lives to make them count?' So they follow Bill Gates' footsteps and move into philanthropy, trying to do something with their money, because they are desperate to make their lives count." He paused only briefly, clearing his throat, and then continued speaking with an even greater urgency, emphasizing the significance of what he was trying to articulate.

"What we do is not just about kids and ministry and Iris in Africa, but it's about its implications in the world. The reality of that helps us get past anything that's just church, or for that matter anything that's just humanitarian. We're not a church, not a Bible school; Iris is not about one part. It's not even about Africa. We're just a little bunch. We can't take care of a whole lot of people, but we can be an example. We are really not just a messy operation to the poor in Africa. If that were the case, we could get on television and write books asking for help. We don't do that because the point is to give God credit and we want people to see what He can do. Instead of asking for money, Heidi gives offerings to our guest speakers who are pastors and missionaries from around the world. We turn the tables on them; the whole idea is to turn everything upside down."

The conversation turned then to the Christmas preparations and gifts when Heidi asked one of her assistants if the Christmas gift certificates to the spa had been purchased for the missionaries. One of Heidi's friends had given her a personal gift of money, and she was using that to buy the certificates.

Just before we all said good-bye for the evening, I was warmly invited to attend the staff Christmas party on Christmas Eve, which would be at the Italian restaurant on the beach. They also told me about the feast for the community on Christmas Day, when four thousand kids with their families would come to the center to eat a chicken feast. It would be the highlight of their year.

On the morning of Christmas Day I helped the missionaries pack two hundred gift bags for the kids at the center, which took us almost four hours. After we chose the right sized clothing for each child, we added the toys that were age- and sex-appropriate, and topped it off with large fistfuls of candy. We had to be sure to keep the bags off the floor so the

ants wouldn't get to the lollipops before the kids did, which
was also the reason the organizers had waited until Christmas
Day to pack the bags.

We started early so the bags would be ready for Heidi when
she arrived at around 10:00 a.m. I watched as Heidi personally
handed out the gifts to each child, sitting with them on the
dusty marble-slabbed porch outside of the child's dormitory.
Each dormitory was a long, narrow building with an awning
in the front held up by rough-hewn wooden posts that offered
shade from the hot African sun. Still, sweat dripped down
Heidi's neck, her damp hair swept out of her face by the black
cotton visor she wore. A small group of visitors and missionaries followed Heidi from porch to porch, celebrating with the
kids as they opened their presents. It took seven or eight hours
before they all received their gift bags, but Heidi's enthusiasm
seemed to be the same for the last child as it was for the first.
One of the missionaries standing next to me remarked that
giving and receiving gifts was one of the signature things for
which Heidi was known. She just loved it.

One little boy ran around goofily, bouncing back and
forth like a ping pong ball from one person to the next,
pulling toy after toy out of his gift bag until it was empty.
Then he put everything back into the bag so he could take it
all out again for the next person. The handheld video game
seemed to be his favorite, and he begged everyone to show
him how to play it.

It was the boy's first Christmas at the center, and it seemed
to be his first Christmas ever to receive gifts. When he first
arrived from the bush only a month earlier, everyone thought
he was mute because he didn't say a word for weeks. But now
he was chattering away fluently in Makua (the tribal language
of the region) and Portuguese. His big eyes and innocent,
open face were almost irresistible.

He went again and again to Heidi, hugging her from behind, even when she was already holding another child on her lap. "You're such a cheeky one…you were so shy when you first got here, we thought you didn't know how to speak. Look at you now chattering away," she said to him in English, as she pulled lightly on his arm, which was around her neck. He grinned and ran away, throwing himself onto the back of one of the male missionaries.

After the gifts we all made our way to the kitchen for the chicken, rice, and soda feast. There were Christmas lights strung crazily from the wooden beams of the large rectangular room that had half walls and large openings for windows. As I helped open hundreds of bottles of Coca-Cola and orange Fanta, I especially enjoyed watching the little ones. They sat on the floor instead of on wooden benches at the table, and they ate with their hands because it was easier for them, shoving fistfuls of rice, coleslaw, and chicken into their little mouths. The older kids crunched on the chicken bones, chewing them until they could swallow them.

With the kids running and jumping and screaming and eating all at once, it was so noisy that it was difficult to hear the woman next to me when she told me the night before had been just as humid, just as loud, and just as chaotic (and nothing like the quiet, contemplative Christmas Eve service she was used to in her home country of Australia). She pointed out the few teenage boys who were still carrying around the little candles from the previous night's candlelight service. Most of the kids chased each other, trying to blow out each other's candles. The volunteer told the story with a smile, and I felt as if I had missed out for not attending.

As I walked back to my concrete hut looking at the African stars in the deep midnight sky, I thought about Iris and Rolland and Heidi Baker, humanitarian aid, health care, education for

the poor, and abandoned children finding family. I thought
about things a little less tangible, as Rolland had implied,
things like hope and love, the spirit through which the aid
was given, and how they seemed to be moving like fire across
Mozambique. It was that fire that needed to spread in order
for the poor to have a better quality of life, and I was interested in how they fanned the flame.

Chapter 2

LIFE IN PEMBA

BLONDE-HAIRED, BLUE-EYED HEIDI, who had grown up in Southern California, was not the obvious candidate to be a missionary in a third-world country. She was more likely to go to an Ivy League university like her father and have a successful career in any number of fields. But Heidi and Rolland left the United States more than thirty-five years ago, seeking out the poor and broken in the third world and reaching out to people who lived in obscurity and extreme poverty, and surprisingly the Bakers seemed happier than most people I knew who had successful careers in the West. Heidi and Rolland found their own type of success in Mozambique—to them success looked like the hungry being fed, the sick being healed, and orphans finding a family.

Looking out the front metal gate of the Iris compound, called the Village of Joy, the turquoise Indian Ocean shines in the distance, sunshine making the water dance with brilliant glints of shimmering light. Facing the compound from the gate, Iris looks like its own village. The property is too big to see the whole thing at once. The buildings, simple concrete block structures, are situated neatly on the hill, which gradually continues up beyond the eye's reach. Some of the buildings are open-air, meaning they had roofs but big cut-outs for windows with no screens. But in Africa what goes on inside the structure is always more notable than the architecture itself.

I was overwhelmed by how many projects went on at once

in the Village of Joy. There was a milk program for nursing babies whose mothers didn't have enough breast milk to feed them. The baby house cared for thirty abandoned or orphaned babies and toddlers. The lunch program fed close to a thousand very hungry kids from the village. There was a primary school for two hundred adopted Iris children plus more than a thousand kids from the village, a new secondary school, a Bible school for three hundred Mozambicans from rural areas, and a cross-cultural missions school for three hundred international students who were from all over the world.

There was also a well-drilling program that provided clean water wells for needy villages in Mozambique, a prison ministry that took food and basic-needs items such as soap and toothbrushes to inmates in both the prison and town jail, health clinics for the community to receive free health care and medicine, public health teaching in the local churches, and programs for widows to receive food and housing for their vulnerable families. Each program was full-time work for a whole team of people.

The absolute enormity of all that happened each day in Pemba, not to mention at the other Iris bases around the world, was the main reason Heidi was stretched thin. She had very little time for herself. With all the international travel she did, her body had no idea what time it was, so sleeping more than four or five hours a night was usually impossible. She often felt that she didn't have time to sleep anyway; there was legitimately too much to do. Heidi often missed meals because she was in a meeting or speaking or out in the village with people who did not have enough food.

Though the events of the week often appeared to outsiders to be disorganized, Heidi had a weekly rhythm in Mozambique. Sunday, the first day of the week, began early with a church service of about two thousand people—villagers from the surrounding areas, the two hundred children who lived at the Village of Joy, and the many international guests (sometimes as many as four hundred at a time), which included the missions school students. When the music started, everyone gathered in the open-air concrete and metal church building that had replaced the green-and-white-striped tent where they used to gather to worship. Some of the teenagers led the upbeat singing and played accompanying instruments while five or six young adult men from the community led the energetic line dancing at the front of the platform. The African dance was energetic and alive. Even in one-hundred-degree heat or in a mud hut, the worship transformed the atmosphere.

The African form of worship was different from anything I'd experienced in the West. The music and dancing were community-oriented, and no one felt alone or awkward. It was a microcosm of Mozambican culture, where everyone was included, everyone was part of the family. In this culture everyone could dance; everyone could sing, no matter how off key. Success wasn't judged by how skillful someone was but on whether he participated.

The music eventually became less energetic and more devotional; passionate, it focused on cries from the heart. Then Heidi usually preached the sermon in Portuguese, and it was translated into English and Makua, a local African dialect. If there was an English-speaking guest speaker, he or she preached in English and the message was translated into the other two languages. It was quite the international community, with people in attendance from all over the world. This meant the message had to be cross-cultural and relevant to a wide range of people, those from the African bush village as well as city slickers from the Western world.

Church in Pemba was an overload for the senses, and I wondered if I would ever grow accustomed to the intense heat, all the greetings (it was customary to say hello and perhaps even stop to talk to every single person you knew) or the cacophony of noises: the sometimes-off-key harmonies, feet pounding the concrete floor, hundreds of small children running and screaming in the middle of everything.

Eva was a seventeen-year-old American girl who came from a wealthy suburb on the East Coast to do a three-week internship before she started her senior year of high school. She planned to study medicine, as both of her parents had successful careers in medicine. Raised in a different religious tradition, Eva worried that she would feel out of place or at the worst end of the spectrum maybe even be persecuted for her different faith background. Iris was, after all, a Christian organization; she wondered if she should even go on the internship. She had heard about Iris from a colleague of her father's, whose best friend was volunteering in Mozambique. Her father's colleague assured her that nothing would be forced upon her and that she and her different beliefs would be respected.

The hospitality team met her at the airport, escorting her to her room in the visitor's center on the base. Eva had already made a friend on the plane: an older Scottish woman who was also going to visit Iris for two weeks. During the orientation Eva was told that she didn't have to attend church in the morning. "OK," she said. On Sunday morning I saw her walking to the church building with a group of others.

"You don't have to go to church," I reminded her.

"I know," she said. "I just want to see what it's like."

The preacher was a female speaker visiting from Canada. She spoke about the forgiveness and restoration that Jesus's suffering on the cross accomplished for us so that we could draw close to Him instead of being distanced by our sin.

When the service ended just after noon, Eva was with the rest of the crowd leaving the building. I was surprised she had stayed for the whole service. "So, what did you think?" I asked her, concerned that the message may have offended her.

"I liked it! It's really vibrant; there's so much going on. It wasn't boring at all. And everyone is so loving!" she said, as if surprised.

Some Christians would consider Eva's lack of an immediate outward conversion a failure, but Heidi and those who worked with her knew that planted seeds could be watered at any time. Sometimes the journey to salvation took time. Continuing to show love and stay in relationship showed more about the heart of God than pressuring someone to make a decision for Christ when they weren't ready.

Every Sunday evening Heidi had a gathering at her house, which was a mile or so away from the Iris base. Heidi always invited about ten kids, ten youth, ten missionaries, and ten international visitors. It felt a little like a mix between a huge family dinner and a birthday party. Sometimes we did celebrate birthdays or special occasions, like going-away parties or bridal showers.

Near the beginning of my time in Mozambique, Heidi's son, Elisha, was visiting for his birthday, so Sunday night became a celebration for him. The atmosphere was both jovial and intimate. The sloping yard, covered by a tree canopy, was lit by glowing yellow candles fit neatly into containers decorated with white crystallized sea salt. Missionaries and Mozambican staff dressed up, the women wearing their best dresses. Some of the younger girls gathered together before the party to get ready together, as if preparing for a high school dance, asking each other questions about makeup and hair and clothes.

Heidi's simple house was inviting, welcoming in the same way she welcomes.

"Hello," she gushed, "I didn't know *you* were here," she said, seeming pleased to see me. She wore a simple, flowing dress.

It seemed she was constantly being stopped by people wanting to talk with her, especially the visitors from the West.

It was Elisha's twenty-fourth birthday. After the dinner (consisting of chicken, goat, coleslaw, and other specialties the Mozambicans eat on special occasions) was served in the same large pots used to feed people at the center, a huge chocolate cake decorated with cherries and pale chocolate icing was set in the center of the table on the front porch.

Heidi stood to lead the birthday song in Portuguese. She laughed as we all sang, her eyes sparkling like a child's. She clapped energetically as Elisha, along with two other girls whose birthdays are also in the month of June, blew out the tiny, flickering candles. Elisha was quiet but didn't seem embarrassed. Heidi and the kids put chocolate icing on their lips and ran around giggling and kissing people on the cheeks, leaving chocolate *beijo* (kiss) imprints behind. And Heidi, in all of the warmth of the evening, surrounded by friends and family and those who love her, radiated a deep sense of joy and gratitude.

On Sunday nights the ten kids that were invited to the dinner spent the night at Heidi and Rolland's house. This was when the kids raided her refrigerator and ate everything in it. Yogurt and soda were their favorite things. It was one way she could tell who still felt like an orphan and who felt like an adopted son or daughter. Often when new ones came into her house, they were so timid and fearful, looking around worriedly and not daring to take anything from the refrigerator. But when they finally understood that they were loved, accepted, and safe, they knew they could eat whatever they wanted. There were stages of moving from orphan to daughter or son; the true sign of sonship or daughterhood was when they could take just what they wanted out of the refrigerator and didn't think they had to eat everything at once out of fear they wouldn't have food tomorrow. Her grown kids who have been with her for years know that everything she has is theirs.

On Monday mornings Heidi arose at 5:00 a.m. to make the kids eggs for breakfast. It was something she took great pride in, as it enabled her to stay connected to the kids even amidst a busy and overcrowded schedule the rest of the week. After Heidi made breakfast for the children, she drove them to the Iris center in time for school, which began with a weekly chapel service that Heidi led on Mondays at 7:00 a.m.

She catered to the kids with songs they enjoyed singing, even letting some of the children help lead the service. Sometimes she asked them to speak into the microphone about what they wanted to be when they grew up. It was chaotic and loud, with some of the younger children running around screaming and playing tag while their teachers chased them around the building trying to get their attention. It was just the way Heidi loved it: holy chaos, full of life and energy, many things happening at the same time, and very, very free.

At 8:00 a.m. the children left for their classrooms, which were situated on the base at the top of the hill. As the children were leaving, the widows from the villages were just arriving at the church for their weekly discipleship time. One of Heidi's priorities was meeting with the women and encouraging them, and she had assigned one or two of the missionaries and a few of the national staff to work with them daily. They took requests from those who needed houses, clothing, and food, and they ran a program for a few hundred of the widows and abandoned women, who would come to the base every day to make bead necklaces the ministry could sell. In exchange the women received a month's worth of food for themselves and their families.

After the discipleship time in the church, Heidi went into the village to visit some of the women in their homes. She loved being in the dirt, spending her time with the poor. It was where she got the most life, and by visiting the homes of the women, she was able to see which ones were really in dire need and which were merely needy, like most everyone else. Heidi always did her best to act as God would toward the world, meaning she always took it as her responsibility to help anyone in need. She would try to be the answer for the person in front of her even if it meant personal sacrifice. Most days she felt physically tired and hungry. Most days she also felt it was worth it.

Following Heidi's example, I sought out friends in the village, spending a lot of time with Fatima, who was a single mother from the neighboring village. We always sat together in front of her mud hut on a grass mat in the dirt, whiling away the time. This is what she did each day after her daily tasks were finished—she talked to her neighborhood friends as a way to pass the time.

When she walked to the well to get water to carry to her clay storage tank, I followed her, observing typical life in the village. She laughed hysterically when I marveled at the weight she could carry on top of her head. She tried to teach me to balance a large bucket filled with a small amount of water on my head, and then she laughed even harder.

One day, when the sun was high and bright in the sky, I inquired about when they would eat their daily meal. I didn't want my presence to keep the family from eating or for her to feel as if she had to offer me some of her food.

"We're not eating today," she said so matter-of-factly I thought I misunderstood her.

"What do you mean?" I asked.

"We don't have any food today," she stated simply, showing no emotion, as if this was an experience she was used to.

"Why?" I asked confused.

"My brother never stopped by to give us money to buy food, so we don't have anything to eat today." Again her tone was matter-of-fact.

I had no response. I was hoping my horror and sadness wasn't too obvious; I didn't want to offend her. This circumstance was unusual for me, but not for her.

"Let's go to the market," I said.

We journeyed a few miles, through winding dirt lanes and mud huts, up hills, and down rocky paths until we came to the open-air market in the center of the village. Across the hills of the village the ocean shimmered in the distance.

The stench of the fish drying in the hot sun was overpowering, and I wondered how anyone could find those tiny sardines appetizing. I encouraged Fatima to buy whatever she needed for food, and she carefully picked out a small handful of fish and had the vendor measure a few cups of rice. She bought a small bottle of cooking oil, some charcoal for the fire, coconut, a clove of garlic, and a few tiny onions. The cost was less than two dollars. My heart broke at the pitiful amount of what to me was a meager meal.

I thought about the strain of survival, how each day Fatima must have worried about how she was going to get food to feed her children, how this must be the case for not only her but for thousands of others in the surrounding villages, who were lucky if they could eat a couple of times a week.

Back at Fatima's house she made a fire in the dirt outside her one-room mud hut. After preparing and cooking the food over the charcoal fire, she sat on the ground on the straw mat and chose the smallest plate out of the plastic plates of food she had dished out. A neighbor who spoke English and Portuguese explained for me: "The mother always takes the smallest because she doesn't want her children to feel they didn't get enough food at home."

A few days later Fatima's adorable two-year-old son, Johnny, was crying from hunger. I discovered Fatima used to have a husband, but he left her for another woman whom he provided for instead. This was not atypical of families and households in the villages of this rural, sun-scorched town in northern Mozambique. Many of the men had more than one wife, abandoning multiple women when they felt like moving on.

I was beginning to understand why Heidi did what she did. These new friends gave me so much more than what I had to offer them. What I was learning about endurance, community, the importance of interdependence, and joy in the midst of suffering were invaluable lessons I would never learn anywhere else but sitting in the dirt with the poor, who I would never classify as "poor" again. They had become my friends. They were no longer nameless and faceless, and through them I realized we all have areas of our lives that are in poverty. I was not their savior; rather we were equals and sisters, both of us having something to contribute to the other, because we were created in God's image.

Heidi appeared to get the most joy from spending time with people way out in distant villages or even just nearby villages that were full of those who were needy. Somehow desperation and neediness are what attracted her most to people. This tendency reflected something she believes about God: He is attracted to our need and really desires to meet those needs. It's as if somehow He has a special place in His heart for the poor and broken, as if He gives them preferential treatment.

This was how Heidi viewed people—the humble and poor were the most special to her, the most deserving of time and attention. It was opposite of the world's system. Everything was upside down in Heidi's system, and yet it produced greater and more fruitful results than anything I'd seen, certainly more than the dry university system I had come from where the theory never led to real and effective practice. Heidi was all about what was real and what was practical, and she had little time for mere words. She preached what she lived—most of her messages were full of stories of what she'd actually experienced.

Monday afternoons, after she returned from the village with promises to build houses for women and their children, Heidi led a meeting with her Mozambican senior staff to plan which village they would visit on outreach from Thursday to Saturday. Every Thursday there were two or three outreach teams of fifteen or twenty people (both internationals and Mozambicans) that went to the surrounding villages to offer food, medicine, and prayer to the poor community. The local pastors kept track of which villages they had not yet visited and which villages they might have already been to but that were still in need of a school, a well, or a church.

Most of these local pastors had gone through the three years of Iris's Bible college. When Heidi first started the Bible school in her early days in Mozambique, she invited poor men and women from the villages to come to the Iris base to live and learn for three months at a time. They didn't have to pay for their housing, food, or schooling. Classes were every day but Saturdays. Then they went back to their families and planted a local church in their town.

By the time I was first hearing about them in 2005, the Iris Bible schools had been in operation for more than ten years and had graduated thousands of students, which meant Iris had thousands of churches (a church consisted of at least twenty-five adults and usually many children). On this Monday afternoon meeting with the local pastors Heidi received updates about these various Iris bush churches, and these updates often dictated decisions made about where they would go for the coming week's outreach.

On Tuesday mornings Heidi held a staff meeting for her national and international staff. She actively tried to encourage the staff each week, and they all listened to updates from the various departments. After the staff meeting she taught at the missions school, where she brought in up to three hundred international students from around the world to learn from her and the Village of Joy model in Pemba. The students usually were so impacted by the time they left Mozambique that many decided to do something completely different with their lives than what they thought they would do before arriving in Mozambique. Their new plans often included giving away, selling, or packing away their material possessions in the West and moving to a third-world nation, where they sought out the most broken in society.

Some of the international alumni moved to Cambodia and Thailand to rescue children from sex slavery; some moved to India to rescue child slaves from the mines. One young girl went to the Congo in search of rebel soldiers to minister to and also started building schools for the children affected by war. Others started a disaster relief branch of Iris. They became the first to get on a plane to an area struck by a natural disaster, bringing whatever resources they could, even dressing up in costumes in the shelters in Japan after the earthquake to bring fun, games, and toys for the kids, and holding and praying for the adults as they wept. The visions of how to change the world were as numerous as people's nine-to-five professions in the West.

Heidi always said her least favorite part of her job was the huge amount of administration the ministry required. Usually even her free time was taken up with administrative meetings. Many afternoons she had meetings scheduled back to back, often running until ten or eleven in the evening. Sometimes, if she were lucky, someone would bring her a cold plate of rice and beans to the meetings near lunchtime.

Wednesdays were completely devoted to administration, when Heidi scheduled meetings and took phone calls from around the world to deal with pressing issues in other countries where there were Iris bases. Often the Iris base leaders needed counsel or advice and sometimes they even had requests for money. Her former base in the south of Mozambique was once fined almost $100,000 for not getting their hiring procedures and salaries quite right according to the government. On Wednesdays it was not uncommon for Heidi to meet with her assistant (who helped her tackle the admin) for nine hours without a break, and even still the next day there would be more administrative work waiting.

On Thursday mornings Heidi taught the Bible school students and then the missions school students, interacting with a total of six hundred of them, sometimes at the same time, translating from English to Portuguese or vice versa in the same class. Watching her teach fluidly in two languages to two very different groups of students was a little mind-boggling. Most of the students weren't even aware of how hard this would have been to any other teacher because she made it seem so effortless. Often Heidi appeared almost childlike in her straightforward and genuine approach; the real skill level of what she did was hidden underneath the veneer of simplicity.

I hadn't even gotten through a full week in Heidi's schedule yet, and I was stunned by the pace at which Heidi lived. As

I observed her in action in Pemba, I would sometimes leave her side to take a short break after three or four hours of the intensity of people and events and meetings that she participated in for twelve to fourteen hours a day.

On Thursdays, when she finished teaching her classes, Heidi packed her Land Rover with sleeping bags and tents strapped to the top and squeezed at least ten people into the vehicle to travel to a village for outreach. The selected village was sometimes hours away, and because the sun went down around five o'clock each night, often much of the drive was in the murky darkness, the vehicle bouncing up and down over the dirt roads. On the way out of town Heidi always pulled into the gas station to fill up the tank and buy snacks for everyone: potato chips, cashews, and sodas. It would be a long time before they ate a real meal, though later that evening there might be spaghetti cooked over the fire and mixed with canned tuna.

Despite the hardships of these weekly trips—time away from the children, little food or rest, and less time for administrative tasks—Heidi went every week. Outreach was one of her favorite parts of the week, she told me. She really desired to know the villagers, and that meant she sat with them in the dirt, shared her food with them, and always stayed overnight, usually sleeping in a tent in a dirt field.

Only ten days after I arrived in Africa, I went on an outreach to a village about thirty minutes away. Heidi was away, speaking at a conference somewhere in the Western world, so the local pastors were in charge of the logistics. The road was deep red and dusty. About twenty of us, fifteen Westerners and five Africans, rode in the back of a truck, bouncing along over the potholes and ducking as we passed low tree branches.

We passed shacks made from mud and stopped at the edge of a piece of barren land that stretched for miles into the horizon of the trees. On the other side of the barren field were the villagers' mud houses and a bathroom that was simply a deep hole in the red earth surrounded by a stall made from tall reeds. The reeds reminded me of the labyrinths I grew up making from corn stalks in the autumn season, and I thought it ironic: necessity versus entertainment, the polar opposites of the third world and the first world.

Hundreds came running and screaming toward us. For some of the kids it was their first look at a person with light skin. "*Acuna* (white person)," they shouted, pointing. The small girls laughed at everything, and they were delighted to give me a high-five. They slapped my hand palm down and then jumped up and down, giggling and clapping.

I observed a group of twenty boys and girls staring at two of the white girls who had gotten tired and hot and sat on the back of the truck. The kids were captivated by the girls' long hair, facial features, and light eyes.

I filmed the children's surprise, their openness, their receptivity, their delight in simple gifts such as stickers and bubbles. They loved looking at themselves in the video camera. They were on the screen, and they were moving. They had never seen anything like it, and had no concept of television or cameras; most of the children had never even seen themselves in a mirror.

I joined the two girls on the truck after an hour or so, and one played the guitar while we sang. We had a small audience of about fifty kids, and I felt like we were performing. The girl complained that the guitar was missing a string, but realizing the villagers didn't know the difference, we continued.

Shortly afterward, the Mozambican pastor who came with us started to speak to the crowd. There were lights and microphones powered by the generator we brought, and he spoke loudly into the microphone, telling the people how his father wanted to kill him because he had left his family's faith and was now a Christian, but he didn't care; this love was worth it all.

Some rushed to the front of the truck when he told them Jesus still heals and asked if they wanted prayer for sickness. They were desperate for healing, with no medicines and many sicknesses. One boy had discernible pink eye; he held my hand while I tried not to pull away. It seemed cold and selfish to reject his love merely because I didn't want to catch his sickness.

I stayed back watching. I was told these were the moments when healings and miracles occurred, but I was tired and cold and very hungry since we had missed dinner. So I sat in the truck trying to get warm and looked forward to going back to the base to get something to eat. From where I sat, I could see everything, and it didn't look like much was happening.

The next morning at breakfast one of the girls who had been singing with us to the children claimed that everyone for whom she prayed was healed, including those suffering from back pain and a boy who was deaf. She asked the interpreter to tell her what happened with the boy.

"He's fine; he can hear," the interpreter said. "Let's move on to the next person."

"It was incredible," she said with her South African accent.

But I was not sure. I thought perhaps she had missed something in the language and cultural barrier and that some things were lost in translation. I doubted because I had not seen it with my own eyes, and the girl had been so eager to see the miraculous that she claimed the dust particles in the pictures on her digital camera were angels. Later Rolland told me the "orbs" that show up in pictures are simply lens flare easily caused by bright lights in dark situations.

I wanted to believe in miracles; it's just that I had never seen one. There were, of course, those moments when I wondered if

I had witnessed a miracle, but nothing as tangible as the deaf hearing or the blind seeing, which seemed to be a common occurrence in the Iris world.

The following week, just after New Year's Day in 2006, Heidi returned from her trip and invited me to go on an outreach with her. When we arrived at the village, the villagers were already watching *The Jesus Film* in their own language (an Iris team had gone ahead of Heidi's car to set up the equipment and start the film). In *The Jesus Film* there were scenes of Jesus multiplying bread so the hungry had more than enough, and Him watching with pleasure as His disciples pulled in a large catch of fish from the sea. The ones surrounding us— the poor, the hungry, the sick—could understand and receive Jesus's message with a simplicity lacking in Western culture. They were eager to receive bread, healing, and love.

As the film played, we set up our tents in the dirt outside the pastor's hut. When we were finished, we went to the back of the flatbed truck, which had been turned into a platform, and Heidi called the sick forward so she could pray for them. People told me many were healed each week at this time on outreach. I didn't know how to take this when I first arrived in Mozambique, but I stopped myself from drawing a conclusion and hoped to see a miracle with my own eyes.

I went on the outreach with Heidi with my senses awake, determined not to let tiredness or hunger or the cold night air pull me away from witnessing the deeper things that might be happening. As she prayed for the sick and then preached about God's love for the people, I stood close, taking pictures with my digital camera, wanting to catalog and remember this place that was so different from anywhere I had ever been. It was a different world.

As I looked at the second or third photo on my camera, I noticed what looked like burning orange and red flames leaping out of the photo. I took another photo, and again, the same thing happened.

Click, click, click—in picture after picture the flames appeared, each time in different places on the photo depending on the angle I used. One flame appeared behind Heidi's back, like an angel's wing. It was the oddest thing, and I had no rational explanation for it.

Someone told me that others who had been on outreaches in the past had experienced the same phenomenon in their pictures. Rolland later explained that the "flames" could be reproduced. Small pocket cameras set at "auto" with the flash turned on at night left the shutter open for longer exposures. When the flash went off, the image froze. Because the flash light was cold and the other lights that showed up during a longer exposure were much warmer, orange streaks that happened to look like flames were produced. Despite Rolland's explanation, I still couldn't shake the unnerving feeling the images gave me, and how similar they seemed to the flames of fire the early believers saw.

On one outreach I tossed and turned all night on a straw bed that wasn't long enough for my five-foot-four frame. I noticed Heidi tossed and turned too; we were in a mud hut that the people had built for her as a thank-you for building a school for them. At four or five in the morning, I noticed Heidi sit up in the dark, pour something into her water bottle, shake it, and drink the whole thing before laying back down. In the morning I noticed a Starbucks Via packet on the ground. It made me laugh. Even she, one of the best missionaries on the planet, was desperate for a pick-me-up after a night in a mud hut.

In the morning we drank more coffee and ate scrambled eggs cooked over the fire. Then we promptly had a worship service, which included a wedding ceremony for a couple who didn't have the resources to have one performed by a government official. Then Heidi worked with her team to draw up rudimentary plans to build a school building, which would function as a church building on Sundays.

Often on outreaches the villagers sent Heidi away with chickens, goats, or fruit as offerings and gifts, the kids jumping and grinning as she drove away, feeling as though they were not forgotten and that someone important cared for them. She genuinely did.

It was late Friday evening when Heidi arrived home from outreach. She stopped at the center first to drop off her guests who had traveled all the way from the United States, Australia, England, or another first-world nation to see her work in Mozambique.

One Mozambican man waited for Heidi at the gate of the Iris compound, calling for "Mama Aida" as she was driving out of the center. Even though she was in a rush, already late for her dinner appointment, she rolled down the window to talk to him and then discreetly gave him a handful of cash to fix the caved-in roof on his house.

"Stopping for the one" was one of her life's messages, and she always tried to stop, even and especially when it was inconvenient. Because of her intense schedule, it often was.

Saturday was supposed to be Heidi's day off, though it rarely happened that she was actually able to take time off. Perhaps she didn't say no enough or perhaps it was due to others' heavy demands on her, but someone was always there with a need or was just desperate to be close to her.

One Saturday morning an American woman Heidi didn't know arrived at her back door. Heidi's guard had let her in the gate, figuring she was a friend or coworker just because she was white. The woman had arrived in Mozambique just an hour or so before. At the airport she met the Iris hospitality team that was picking up their scheduled guests. When the woman told them she was also coming to stay at Iris, the director of hospitality kindly told her that he didn't have her on his list; he asked her if she had applied.

"No," she said, "God told me to come, and I got on the plane."

"I'm sorry, Miss, but God didn't tell us you were coming," he replied, tongue-in-cheek. "We are a children's center, so we carefully screen our visitors. You will have to stay at a hotel, but you're welcome to come to church on Sunday. We'll be happy to take you to the hotel across the road."

The woman grumbled and complained and then yelled at him, trying to guilt him into taking her to the center, but he refused to cave. The woman promptly went to the beach to interrogate the teenage vendors about where "Mama Aida" lived. As they led her to Mama Aida's house, they told her all kinds of stories about what they needed, what she should give to them, and sad stories about their lives—and they said Heidi wouldn't help them. This was a way to manipulate the woman into giving them what they wanted.

This gave the woman the ammunition she was looking for, and she stormed into Heidi's house on her day off, accusing her of not helping the street boys and saying Heidi shouldn't call herself a Christian if she didn't help those boys in need. She also yelled at Heidi about her staff and how they prevented her from staying at the center. Heidi was flabbergasted. She didn't know who this woman was or how she had gotten to her house. It took Heidi a few minutes to react at all as the woman stood there yelling and glaring at her like a bull ready to charge.

"It's OK, sweetie," she said, trying to calm the woman down. "We do help the boys, and we'll help you too. Let me take you to your hotel; it'll be my joy to pay for your stay there." By the time Heidi got the woman settled, it was late into the afternoon and any chance she had of a quiet and reflective day of rest diminished like the clear sky dissipates in Mozambique's rainy season, the black clouds building and gathering.

The next morning Heidi would wake up and repeat the weekly rhythm of life in Mozambique, with all its demands and challenges, discomforts and joys.

Chapter 3

THE GIFT OF HEALING

IRACLES AND PHYSICAL healings were a common part of Heidi's ministry, and I was curious to witness these. This was my first time in a developing country where extreme poverty was routine and there was just one doctor for every thirty-three thousand people, as was the case in Mozambique. The sick had no choice but to believe that God could heal them without the intervention of medicine. During my time in Mozambique I realized that faith was just as much a choice as doubt.

On my third outreach I struggled to comprehend what happened and how it happened when I saw a deaf mute boy hear and then speak. The evidence was there, but the generator's lights were hot and bright against the dark African sky, the noise of the people was jarring, and though I saw his lips move and his eyes widen in surprise, I didn't hear his voice at first.

Everyone who worked with Heidi seemed to be used to this kind of thing and talked about miracles as if they were routine, because they happened so often.

During this particular outreach, soon after we arrived on the back of the truck, Heidi asked the village if they knew anyone who was deaf. "Bring them here," she said, looking out into the crowd of people who had gathered around. They stood in the dirt field. The women wore cloth wrap skirts, the colored print faded from washing and rewashing and line drying in the tropical sun. The children were dirty, and their clothes had holes in them from being passed down from child to child.

One of the mothers pushed a young boy named Abilio to the front, and Heidi pulled him onto the truck bed beside her. She put her hands on his ears, closing her eyes, then she pulled him into an embrace and held him there against her heart, rocking him slightly. They stayed that way for a long time while I looked on. It seemed such an intimate moment that I didn't want to intrude in any way, but I was trying to figure out how Heidi did what she did. I was analyzing her, but love is something to be experienced rather than analyzed.

Suddenly Heidi pulled away slightly from the boy to look him in the eyes. Her eyes were shining. She spoke to him in his own language, saying something similar to "*Oluco orreira* (God is beautiful)." The nod of his head was almost imperceptible, but Heidi grinned, taking his hand and putting it to her throat so he could feel her vocal chords as she said it again. "*Oluco orreira.*"

She looked at me, smiling. "Can you imagine being able to hear for the first time since birth?" she asked. It's as if she knew I was observing, desperate to understand. I had expected the equivalent of lightning bolts, but this was as simple as an embrace, a mother holding a child.

I shook my head. *No, I can't.*

She held the boy's fingers to her throat as she spoke, and then to his own throat, teaching him. She also tried to teach his older brother to teach him. Abilio's brother sat behind him, but then Heidi moved Abilio away from his brother so he couldn't see or feel him. "Clap," she told his brother.

Behind Abilio's head the older boy placed his hands together and clapped loudly. Abilio turned to look, his head whipping around to find the source of the noise. We all laughed with delight. It was obvious he responded to the sound.

The next day Abilio came by himself to our compound; he had never been there before. Almost immediately he saw

me under the green-and-white-striped circus tent and he ran
to me. Then when he recognized Heidi, I heard him speak:
"*Acuna* (white person)," he said half-whispering and pointing
to Heidi, the sound of his voice raspy and uncertain. His face
was close to mine as he whispered and his eyes were wide, as
if still surprised by the sound of his own voice.

Because he never used his vocal chords before, his voice
was gravelly. As he was still learning the power of one voice,
his voice, I was learning the deafening sound of a whisper
and the way it could change everything about the way one
saw the world.

This experience opened me to the possibility that there was
much more to life than what I was seeing. I was beginning to
suspect what I saw with my natural eyes and perceived with
my senses was nothing more than the tiny tip of an iceberg,
that the largest part lay unseen, mostly hidden, but gigantic
and shining and beautiful in its hiddenness.

Later when I asked Heidi whether miracles happened often
when she prayed, her answer was simple: "Not as often as I
would like."

Then she told me about the time a woman in a wheelchair
was healed. Heidi was being interviewed for a Christian television station, and after her interview the driver picked her up
to take her back to her hotel. He had a small request.

"Will you please pray for my mother?" he asked.

"Of course," Heidi said. She never wanted to turn anyone
away, and she went out of her way to be kind, even when it
meant her own discomfort. The driver explained that his
mother had been in a wheelchair (though Heidi no longer
remembers the specific illness because she has prayed for so
many people).

What she does remember is the pile of Kleenexes left in her
hotel room after the man and his mother left the room and

the wheelchair. Who could forget that—a wheelchair left in your hotel room? The woman got up out of her wheelchair and walked up and down the hall. In all of her excitement she left her wheelchair in Heidi's room. She thanked Heidi, and perhaps she realized she was leaving the wheelchair behind and didn't want to see it again. Maybe faith was at work, because many have wondered in their doubt if perhaps healing was only a temporary thing: *Maybe tomorrow or a month from now, I will need it again. Maybe, just to be safe, I should take it with me.* Perhaps the woman knew her wheelchair was the symbol of her imprisonment and leaving it in Heidi's room was a sign of her freedom. Or maybe in all of her excitement, she merely forgot it. Her wheelchair and the pile of used tissues from all the tears of joy are the vivid images Heidi sees when she remembers that moment.

"I can tell you about another time when God healed a quadriplegic," Heidi said, as if the images of the wheelchair and tissues weren't sufficient. "I was in a meeting in Brazil, and there were thousands of people kneeling and on their faces because God's presence was so tangible. I couldn't stand up to speak. No one could stand," she explained. She had been on her face the whole time. Even when she had spoken, she had put the microphone to her lips while she continued to lie on the floor prostrate. "A young couple crawled up to me where I was lying on the floor."

"There's a young man who's a quadriplegic. Would you please come and pray for him?" they asked her.

She asked Jesus about this young man, and she heard Him say yes.

"Yes, I'll pray for him," she answered.

Heidi crawled down the stairs of the platform feet first, crawling over and around some of the people. Then she saw him, the young man who was quadriplegic. He had flat hands.

They were the first detail she noticed. He had no muscle tone; his body was completely atrophied, his hands and his legs flat like a board. He couldn't speak. He could only blink, and he moved his eyelids enthusiastically.

This young man was in his early twenties, and she could see how he could be really handsome. Heidi felt an incredible rush of love and compassion for him.

"Would you like to get up and walk with me? Would you like to walk home tonight?" Heidi asked him.

Tears rolled down his face.

Heidi remembers praying something very simple, more like a declaration than a typical prayer. She said, "In Jesus's name"—three words that held worlds of possibilities. She understood the authority she had because she believed Jesus had died not only for salvation but also for healing. He taught us to pray, "Your kingdom come here on earth as it is in heaven," and in heaven, there was no sickness. Bodies were perfect.

They were the first two people to stand in the whole meeting. In the room of thousands of people, Heidi and the young man stood up, and he started walking.

She walked beside him slowly. Then he started running. They ran together, holding hands. Then they were leaping and dancing, and all of the people saw what had happened. The ones who didn't know were quickly informed and the whole place erupted with shouts of ballistic joy. They screamed for a long time afterward. There was no other way to express radical joy. It was what stadium crowds did at the most intense, exciting, or joyful moments of sports games, but this was so much more—it was a young man's life changed forever.

"It was the most incredible thing watching him," Heidi said. "That was an amazing night. I'll never forget it as long as I live. God literally healed him."

After the meeting ended, Heidi's hosts escorted her to her

vehicle. The driver drove her all night in order to get her to the next place on her itinerary by morning. Heidi could not contain her tears. "I sobbed for hours in the back of the van," she told me. "I was filled with the most amazing gratitude and amazement at the beauty of God. He was real and He cared enough to intervene in our broken lives." She thought about His power and how He could use little people like her. She wanted to see a lot more of that.

———

One of the first times Heidi saw God heal in a spectacular way was not long after she had moved to Mozambique. One of the first Mozambicans Heidi partnered with was Miguel, who soon became Pastor Miguel at the Iris center in Maputo. When he married, Heidi performed the ceremony. The wedding was beautiful: the sun was shining, the humidity was low, and everyone was dressed in their best clothes. The bride was radiant. Over a thousand people attended, and they all thoroughly enjoyed the dancing and celebration.

Days after the wedding, however, everyone got terribly sick. Many of the kids started vomiting and didn't stop. The Mozambican men who helped at the Iris base got deathly sick too. Heidi and Rolland spent most of their time driving people to the hospital, sometimes taking ten to fifteen kids at a time. When the doctors examined them, they determined the kids had cholera, and the infected kids and adults had to be taken to a tent outside of the city.

The doctor from the department of health was furious with Heidi, and Heidi had to keep seeing her as she brought more and more kids to the hospital to be examined and then to the tent filled with the dying. "You're going to kill half of Maputo with this; this is your fault," the doctor spat at Heidi, shaking her finger at her.

All Heidi could do was pray. She wept and prayed. "Please, God. Help! These are Your children too. Show me what to do." As she cried, she saw a picture of herself visiting the children inside the tent, holding them cheek-to-cheek, heart-to-heart.

After that vision Heidi knew she needed to go inside the tent, but no one was allowed to enter. Heidi called Serafino, a Mozambican colleague, who agreed to go with her. Heidi and Serafino looked at each other when they saw the guards at the door; the guards had AK-47s over their shoulders, and they knew they weren't supposed to let anyone in or out. Cholera was a deadly disease and also highly contagious. No one was to get through those doors—it was more off-limits than the emergency room.

When the guards saw Heidi, they smiled and welcomed her. She and Serafino walked right in, hiding their surprise and acting as if they belonged there.

"*Olá*, Mama," the guards said, even opening the tent flap for her. It felt like supernatural favor as they walked on through into the dying room, but what they saw on the other side of the tent flap broke their hearts.

There were over eighty kids and adults squeezed into the space. Each one lay on a wooden board with a hole in it and a bucket underneath. The bucket was to catch the diarrhea: they were so weak they couldn't get up to go to the bathroom. The kids were severely dehydrated as a result, and many of their eyes were sunken in. Hydration was important, but in a country like Mozambique there was no way the necessary equipment would be available for rehydration. No other medical people were there; there was no treatment or medication for cholera.

It looked like a refugee camp for the dying. Heidi's heart broke when she saw Juma, an incredible boy Heidi took home from the streets and loved into her family. She picked him up and held him against her heart as she had done when she first met him. She rocked him in her arms. He vomited on her, but still Heidi continued to pray.

She picked up the little girl in the next bed, who was soiled and smelled, but Heidi held her too, not caring when the excrement soiled her clothes. She could feel love radiating from her, and she was now convinced by the extreme compassion she was experiencing that God would do something. Serafino followed her lead and held each child while he prayed for him.

About halfway through their time in the tent the doctor from the health department came in. She had on a mask, boots, and was fully covered in a protective gown. "You idiot, you idiot! What are you doing? You're going to die, don't you know? They're all going to die, and you're going to die! What are you thinking? What are you doing?" The woman was frantic.

Heidi looked at her calmly: "I'm going to live and not die, and so is everyone in this room."

The doctor was furious that Heidi and Serafino were already completely contaminated, but she didn't make them leave because it was too late. Full exposure had already occurred.

"You're nuts," she mumbled, walking away.

One by one, Heidi fully embraced every child until she had touched each one. Then she moved on to the adults, even the ones she didn't know who must have been guests of the bride. She hugged them close to her heart, holding them in her arms and resting her cheek against theirs as she had seen in the vision. She felt such peace and joy. She felt Love Himself radiating through her and into them and knew something was happening. He was *God*—the definition of goodness and compassion and healing.

Hours later, after they had visited each person in the tent, they left for a few minutes to fetch juice and cookies for the kids. Heidi knew these small treats would make a tremendous difference to their emotional states.

The next day, when Heidi went back to visit, twenty of her kids were standing there waiting for her. They had recovered overnight! They were ready to go home. She was overjoyed.

The day after that another group of kids and adults got up, having recovered their strength. By the third day the room cleared out, and not one person in what the doctor called "the dying tent" died.

The following week the doctor came to find Heidi at the Iris base.

"Your God is God," she said with tears in her eyes. "I didn't believe it, until I saw Him heal those children. I want to work with you," she said simply.

At times people treated Heidi like a celebrity. Even so, it was not the admiration of people that motivated Heidi. It was the fact that there were people in need—broken, hurting, poor, empty, desperate people—that encouraged her to keep going at such a radical pace.

Heidi told me that she used to wish to be a monk, alone in her cell in contemplative prayer and worship. As it is, she spends so much of her time meeting the practical needs of people that she feels she doesn't get enough time alone. A unique blend of Jesus-lover and humanitarian, Heidi did not think that one or the other was sufficient. One of her favorite teachings was "fruitfulness flows from intimacy," meaning that anything we could do for people or the world that was beneficial would directly come out of intimacy with God, knowing Him and His love for us and others.

Once Heidi had a vision of a room in heaven that was full of body parts. Eyeballs opened and closed, blinking at her.

She saw ears and human hearts and gallbladders and tongues; they were all on shelves. When she saw this vision, God said to her, "When I tell you, you can have access to this room."

Heidi knew this was a gift of healing and that she could have access to healing for sick people. When she asked God why she couldn't have access to this room all the time, He answered her: "Because you would never sleep."

Chapter 4

DEVELOPING MOZAMBIQUE

A T THE END of my four months in Mozambique, in the spring of 2006, I realized that my time in Mozambique wasn't over. Heidi and her work had impacted me deeply. I had become a house mom to a group of eight little girls in the children's center, who were seven and eight years old. As a former foster child myself I felt that on a foundational level I understood them and how they felt when they found themselves orphaned or abandoned in some way. They became little sisters to me; they were like daughters. I had developed loving and rich friendships with missionaries and Mozambicans, and I was more inspired by the work they did than by my teaching career. I knew I hadn't even scratched the surface of what I needed to discover in Mozambique, and there was still a book to be written.

I informed the university where I had been teaching that I was staying in Mozambique indefinitely. At the end of 2006 I went to London to the School of Oriental and African Studies to formally study the field of international development, and I returned to Mozambique nine months later, in the summer of 2007, for further research. It was at this time that I met my future husband, Steve, who was attending Iris's three-month missions school and who also happened to be from my home state of Pennsylvania.

After the summer, though my heart was still in Mozambique, I had run out of funds, and I returned to the university in Pennsylvania to teach for a one-year appointment. Steve also returned to Pennsylvania a few months later, and we dated, got engaged, and then married in Philadelphia.

It was mid-2008 when Steve and I decided to return to Mozambique to work with Heidi full time. She needed more help than ever now.

In the early part of 2007 Rolland began losing his short-term memory. At the time, the doctor diagnosed him with post-traumatic stress disorder (PTSD) from his latest trip to the Congo, where his friends had been murdered and their limbs chopped off and sent in boxes to their family members. The doctor ordered Rolland to stop all work and travel. This meant he also had to give up flying his small Cessna plane, which was a great passion of his.

For months he stayed in California, trying to rest and heal. When he returned to Mozambique in the summer of 2007, he immediately came down with cerebral malaria. He returned again to the States for treatment for the life-threatening disease, and he spent almost a month in the intensive care unit. Friends and family were thrilled when he finally returned to Pemba, but Rolland quickly deteriorated, walking around with a blank, glassy look in his eyes, a mere shell of his former self.

Even with Rolland so ill, Heidi continued her work. She was still doing outreaches, still feeding children, and now she was doing most of the administrative tasks Rolland had done.

Heidi took Rolland with her as much as possible. It was easy to take him with her to the church, where people laid out a grass mat for him to lay on. When Heidi brought him along to meetings, church services, or other events, Rolland always lay on his mat, as if he were physically sick. Yet as it turned out, Rolland's main issue was not PTSD but dementia, a disease that causes problems with thinking and memory.

After all the miracles Heidi had witnessed, the one Rolland needed was slow to come.

Rolland slept eighteen—sometimes twenty—hours a day. Some days it was hard for Heidi to get him out of bed at all. Her worry sometimes gave way to frustration at the severity of the situation on top of all the other stressors, responsibilities, and needs that came with living in a developing country. This was marriage for better or worse. Rolland was only sixty-one, but Heidi, who is twelve years his junior, had become his primary caretaker, even bathing and dressing Rolland. It seemed he was at the bottom of a black hole, his mind lost to everyone who loved him.

———————

A few weeks after Steve and I returned to Pemba, Heidi took Rolland with us on an outreach. The outreach was to a remote community across a bay, so the group traveled by boat. Though it wasn't technically an island, it was often referred to as one because the lack of roads made it only accessible by boat. Rolland wore a blank look as he boarded the boat, the captain clasping his hand tight, helping him not to trip as he climbed clumsily over the side. Rolland did not look like a sick man. Besides his shoulders slumping over a little, making him look shorter than his six-foot frame, he appeared mostly physically healthy, though he was unusually quiet and did not often look someone directly in the face.

In an attempt to make conversation, I told him I would make him a chocolate cake with chocolate icing when we got back to Pemba. It was his favorite.

"Just don't make it dry, whatever you do," he replied in a slightly sarcastic tone. "There's nothing worse than dry chocolate cake."

We all laughed good-naturedly, as we would with a beloved grandfather who no longer censored what he said. We were just happy he responded; many times Rolland didn't respond even when someone directly addressed him. Rolland loved cake, chocolate bars, and Coca-Cola, so in addition to the vitamins Heidi encouraged him to take every day, she acquiesced to his desire for sweets. It seemed to be the only thing that lifted his spirits.

There were eleven of us on the boat outreach: Heidi and Rolland, me and Steve, and seven others including Heidi's Mozambican staff and friends. As we waited for the others to arrive, I sat on the pier, dangling my feet over the edge into the warm, clear water. From there I had a spectacular view of the coastline and the villages beyond. I wondered what the village on the other side of the bay would be like. They never received visitors and had no contact or communication with the outside world. They were very much tied to their traditional culture, still wrapping strings around some of their babies' waists, arms, and necks, and dedicating them to be witch doctors.

When everyone was finally on the boat, we pulled slowly out of the harbor, waving to one of Heidi's adoptive sons, who was crying on the dock because he was not allowed to come. When he was much younger, he had run away more times than anyone could count, but Heidi always welcomed him back when life got too difficult on the streets. Jordi was not allowed to join us on the boat trip because he had not done any work the previous week. It was one of the first times I had seen him receive a consequence for his actions, and everyone on the boat seemed to agree it was good for him.

Usually Heidi leaned toward what a friend of hers called unsanctified mercy. At the first sign of tears Heidi would typically tell Jordi that it was OK and that he could do what he was asking as long as he didn't do whatever he had done again. This time Heidi acted differently; it was as if she was making an effort to teach herself that discipline was actually a positive thing to enforce with the children.

A few minutes later all thoughts of Jordi dispersed as we pointed and laughed like children at the dolphins gracefully gliding through the waters and up and over the wake of our boat. When I noticed the bright orange-and-yellow blobs in the water, I wondered if they were coral. Heidi said they were demons; she had once been stung by one of the jellyfish, and it had burned for days.

It took us over an hour to reach the vicinity of the peninsula. The coral reefs flanked the waters, making it impossible to bring the boat close to shore. In order to avoid the shoals, the boat had to stay in deeper water, and we needed to take turns riding the dinghy to shore.

Before we could discuss who would go to the village first, Heidi, determined and eager as a child, was already in the rubber raft, motioning to a few of the local pastors to come with her. They zipped away, waving once to us, then turning around quickly to wave animatedly at the kids on the beach. When the other villagers heard the kids shouting, they flocked to the shore as well, watching the white woman in the rubber boat approach them.

The empty dinghy returned twenty minutes later, and my husband and I encouraged the others to go ahead; we would come last with Rolland. An hour after the dinghy first left, it came back for us. Impatient to join his wife again, Rolland lurched into the boat, losing his balance briefly and almost toppling out of the boat face first into the dinghy. Around his neck was his very expensive camera, so we were worried both for his safety and for his prized camera. He was an expert photographer and editor who had carefully documented Iris's work among the poor in Mozambique.

Steve and I climbed into the boat next and then Alberto, one of Heidi and Rolland's adult Mozambican sons, came behind us. For the past hour the tide had been going out, which meant that now even the dinghy could not make it the whole way to shore.

"Just take us there already," Rolland said, as the boat tacked right then left, as we looked for water deep enough to navigate through.

After five or ten more minutes of trying to inch closer to the shore, Rolland climbed out of the dinghy, throwing one leg over the edge, then the other. It was so fast we didn't have time to respond or tell him why this was a horrible idea.

We doubted that he knew he was walking in the midst of thousands of sea urchins, their black, pointy spikes sticking up out of the shallow water sharper than porcupine needles. Rolland waded through the water unaware of the danger on all sides. Unsteady on his feet, he often lost his balance, lurching forward then backward as he righted himself. We were terrified he would fall into the water, ruining his camera and stabbing himself on the sea urchins.

We sat in the boat, paralyzed for a few seconds, and then called for him frantically to come back, the fear permeating the space around us. When it was apparent that Rolland wasn't going to listen to our pleas for him to return, Alberto, who was wearing water sandals, jumped out of the dinghy, following Rolland, calling out to him.

"Papa Rolland…Papa Rolland, *cuidado! Espera*! (Caution! Wait!)"

When Alberto finally caught up to him, he grabbed Rolland by the arm, steadying him. Steve and I got out of the boat too. The water was too shallow to swim in, and it was dangerous to wade. It was slow going. I stepped on something sharp and cried out from pain. I looked to see what had sliced the sole of my foot: the mangrove root was sharp as it twisted into a point. I was glad it wasn't a sea urchin because they inject venom that can cause complications.

When we finally arrived at the village, the moon was peeking up over the baobab trees. Getting up the long, steep dirt hill upon which the village had built their houses was no easy feat for any of us, especially those of us who were wet, cold, and sticky from the saltwater. The dirt clung to our feet and legs as we climbed and the water still dripped from us, transforming the dirt into a sticky, slippery mud. I was limping slightly from the cut on my foot. The climbing made it hurt worse, but there would be no way to clean it or bandage it until we returned to the mainland the following day.

My husband walked behind Rolland, and when Rolland stumbled backward, Steve steadied him with his hands, half pushing him up the hill. A Mozambican man also saw Rolland lurch backward and, in an effort to help, reached back to pull Rolland toward him. Annoyed, Rolland said, "Someone's pulling me." Steve didn't know what to do but figured it was best to keep pushing him up the hill.

When we arrived, the villagers introduced themselves, asking our names and who was married to whom. We shook the village chief's hand, bowing to him slightly in a gesture of honor as we introduced ourselves one by one. Heidi sat down in the dirt and asked him to tell us about their village. Following Heidi's lead, we all sat. The women went in to the chief's mud hut and brought out their only chairs, three tiny wooden stools, so we wouldn't have to sit on the ground. It was such a thoughtful gesture of hospitality in the dark village, as the night enveloped us and the stars shone like brilliant pinpricks of hope in the night sky. We declined the stools they brought out for us, encouraging the wives of the elders to sit on the stools instead, and they chuckled in embarrassment and amazement.

The village elders told us about the oppression they experienced at the hands of the Portuguese who had colonized Mozambique. During colonial times the people in this village had been enslaved by the Portuguese. After liberation the civil war reached even to their distant land that was almost an island, surrounded on three sides by water. Many were killed.

They related the recent history of a white man who had visited in the last two or three years, who told them he wanted to buy some of their land in order to build a school and a medical clinic; instead, he built a resort that dumped its sewage into the ocean.

"That's horrible," we all murmured in our own ways.

"Did he ever build the school or clinic?" Heidi asked.

When the chief answered sadly that he had not, it was with a tone of resignation, as if there were nothing he could do about it, as if this were to be expected from foreigners. This was the reason Heidi and her team aimed to enter into a village with a certain posture of humility, wanting to serve and learn from the people. This was why we rejected the stools—we wanted to show that we valued them. Heidi was aware that Westerners, even missionaries, sometimes ended up being colonizers. The businessmen were sometimes the worst, when they were eager to maximize their profit no matter the effect on the environment or people or culture.

"As a community, what's your biggest need?" Heidi asked. It was a question she asked the chief of every village. Love looks like something, Heidi always said, and it especially looked like meeting someone's felt need.

There was a lengthy silence before the chief turned to the elders. They talked amongst themselves for some time before answering. "We've never had a school," the chief finally replied, thoughtfully.

He also told us how they had to travel to the mainland

frequently because they had no fresh water anywhere on their land. It took them an entire day and night to reach the mainland by canoe.

The villagers bathed in the sea.

"So, you would like a school?" Heidi asked, repeating what she heard them say.

One of the elders answered by talking further about the water situation; not having a source of fresh water was probably the most difficult thing about their daily lives. It was clear that there was some initial disagreement about which was more important, the school or the water.

"If we have a school, our children can learn and prosper, which will help the whole village," the chief said. The other elders nodded thoughtfully.

"But we need water," one of the men said emphatically.

After some more discussion, the chief made the decision: "We would like a school."

"How do we know that you will really build the school?" he asked.

There was a moment of heavy silence, as it seemed the village leaders were contemplating whether they could trust Heidi and her team. Once they gave her the land, she could build whatever she wanted on it, just as the businessman had done a few years ago.

"We won't be like the man who said he would do something and did something different instead; we want to see your village prosper. We will even bring you the materials so that you can build the school yourselves."

They all began shouting and talking animatedly amongst themselves. As an outsider I couldn't tell if they believed Heidi or not. Was this agreement and excitement or disagreement and doubt? But then they cheered in unison, making the Mozambican sound of joy, singing through their teeth:

"LELELELE." This strangely sweet cacophonous sound was already familiar to me.

When Heidi asked who could sell their land for the school, an old widowed woman volunteered to sell hers, and Heidi paid her the full asking price because she wanted to bless her. The widow could then prosper and buy a bigger piece of farmland.

We made our way back to the boat where we spent the night, camping out on the deck, the air sticky with humidity. It was November, the unbearably hot summer season just starting. We slept with fits and starts, but sleeping on the boat's seat cushions was a bit better than sleeping in a tent on the hard ground.

When we arrived on shore the next morning, we had swimming relays with the kids in the sea. Passing out candy to them afterward, we tried to remember who had already received candy and who hadn't, as the same ones continued to get in line over and over again. We gave up finally, unable to remember the faces of more than a hundred children, and we passed out the candy until the plastic bags were empty. The kids asked for the bags then; nothing was wasted in this culture. It was hard to withhold a few extra pieces of candy from kids who begged for plastic bags.

No one in the entire community had ever been to school. This was common in most rural bush villages in Mozambique, and Heidi related to the people on a simple, basic level. Often it was like relating to children, but most days Heidi enjoyed the simplicity of life in Mozambique.

The plans for the school were drawn up easily as Heidi walked the perimeter of the land with the chief and elders, discussing the elementary structure they would build of bamboo and mud. They were enthusiastic about the tin roof especially, as the local roofs were constructed of dried reeds that needed

to be replaced every few years after the rainy seasons came
and went.

Heidi told them they could use the tin roof to help catch the
rainwater. She described the materials her team would bring
so that they could build a concrete water catchment tank. This
would be a source of fresh water for them. The chief and elders
were thrilled by the idea, and once again, their voices grew
loud and animated.

Heidi had learned almost immediately upon arrival in
Mozambique that time was important to building relationship,
so while the plans took only thirty minutes or so to develop
on a piece of scrap notebook paper that someone had fetched
from who knows where, Heidi spoke with the chief and elders
for over two hours. While they walked from one corner of the
dirt field to the other over and over again in the hot sun, Heidi
asked us if we could play more games with the children.

Through all of the planning and games with children,
Rolland was there. At one point, he wandered away, pacing
back and forth near the trees. He seemed agitated, as if he
were in a hurry to get somewhere. Heidi noticed and walked
over to him to ask if he could speak to the villagers for a few
minutes to encourage them. She led him to the shade of a
tree that was just about as tall as he was, and she asked the
women of the village to gather around. I sat down with the
women on their pieces of cloth fabric, and held my breath as
Rolland stood there silently for a few minutes looking down
at everyone.

"Go ahead, honey," Heidi encouraged him. These days, it
sometimes felt like Rolland was more child than husband.

He launched into a confused monologue about what God
was doing in the world, especially in Asia (the villagers didn't
know where Asia was) and how technology had brought so
many more opportunities (the villagers had no clue what

technology was). One of the guests from Iris looked at me, her eyebrows raised, as if to say, "Oh no!" It was the first time Rolland had tried to preach since the dementia started. It was obvious that he was unaware of his surroundings and his audience. We looked to the women for their reactions, but most of them weren't listening closely at all; most likely they had never been taught about much of anything in a formal way. They had never even had a simple classroom lesson.

Rolland's voice tapered off, and abruptly he quit speaking in what seemed to be the middle of a sentence. He sat down on his mat. Then he lay down. No one in the village seemed to mind that he had started speaking or that he had stopped.

At midday the sun was high and bright in the sky, and it was time for us to head back to the boat so we could arrive home in Pemba before dark. The villagers walked us down the hill to the shore, and we thanked them for their hospitality and waved good-bye. As the dinghy pulled away, they cheered and waved and sang their joyful celebratory chant—LELELELELE—until we were almost out of sight.

When Heidi returned the following week to the village, the old woman who sold her the land for the new school was nowhere to be found, and two government officials met Heidi as she stepped off the small dinghy. They questioned her harshly: "Why didn't you ask for permission to visit this place?"

"There is no way to ask permission. I'm asking for your permission now, if necessary," she responded.

It was obvious they were looking for what they thought would be an easy bribe. They harassed her for almost an hour.

"You cannot build a school here," one of them said.

Heidi was furious when she discovered the government officials had taken the money she had paid the widow. They had treated the old woman roughly, telling her, "You are not allowed to sell land in Mozambique."

The villagers were watching closely the interaction between Heidi and the officials. When Heidi finally realized the officials were not going to change their minds, she turned to the villagers. "If you want this school, you will have to fight for it. If not, I will go home peacefully." She turned and went to wait under a nearby tree. Heidi did not usually challenge the village's chief and elders, but they had allowed the officials to take the money from the widow, and Heidi had already tried to speak diplomatically with the officials, and they weren't budging.

It was unusual that she hadn't been able to win them over. The government officials in these rural bush areas were not better educated than the villagers, and petty bribes were usually their incentives, which meant that anything at all could satisfy them. In the past Heidi had befriended officials with Bibles, solar Bibles, invitations to come to church on Sunday, or offers to teach them English, but these officials just wanted money, and they wanted it badly enough to steal from a widow.

The elders directed the people to the town center where they would talk publicly with the officials. When Heidi heard shouting, she wondered if she should go back to Pemba and return next week. An hour or so passed, and just when she was getting ready to leave, she heard singing.

The officials returned then: "The people have spoken; they will have a school, and they will have a church."

For possibly the first time in their lives, this Mozambican village had fought against corruption and won. So often African governments and those in power simply model the examples they had during colonization. Liberationists taught that violence was the way to fight and overcome. In this case the unified voice of the people was loud enough for the officials to hear.

Heidi smiled sweetly at the officials. "Where is the woman who sold me the land?" she asked.

The villagers told her that the widow was afraid.

"Please bring her to me," Heidi said. "Tell her it's OK. Tell her that she will be safe."

Someone ran away into the village, and when the woman came, she came slowly, haltingly, her head bowed, looking so demoralized she wouldn't even raise her eyes to look at Heidi.

In front of the officials Heidi went to her and hugged her, kissing her on both cheeks, as was the custom. Heidi looked pointedly at the officials before she said to the woman, "I want to give you an offering."

Then she put into the woman's hand the same amount of money she had paid her the first time, plus a little extra. Heidi emphasized again, "This is not payment; this is just an offering."

She looked again at the officials. "This is an offering. This is not payment. Do you understand?" she asked them, waiting until they nodded.

She turned then to the elders and nodded her head once to them to make sure they also understood. The elders would now stand up to the officials and fight for the school, even if it meant defending a widow, someone who, in their society, had very little value.

The poor woman wept loudly, the emotion completely overwhelming her. Eight or nine women snickered at the widow; crying in public was not something people did in their culture. Heidi addressed the group of women directly but gently: "Don't laugh at her. You should rejoice with her. God wants to prosper her, then she can stand up straight with dignity." Heidi wrapped her arms around the woman, holding her as she cried, and one by one, the others all came to stand beside Heidi and gently touch the weeping woman.

As Heidi held her, she empathized deeply with the woman.

In her own life Heidi was still waiting for God to heal her husband.

Part II

EARLY YEARS

Chapter 5

FIRST LOVE

A BLONDE-HAIRED, BLUE-EYED GIRL from Southern California, Heidi seemed unlikely to choose a life of voluntary poverty. Born in Newport Beach, one of the wealthiest areas in the nation, Heidi had what some would call the stereotypical perfect childhood. Her childhood was as good as some are bad: two successful parents, ballet classes, cello lessons, modern dance, modeling, theater, and surfing the California waves.

Heidi's family house was on beachfront property with a private beach for her backyard. The least expensive house in the Laguna Beach area where they lived was worth well over a million dollars, and Heidi says her family house was simple compared to the others. Her father liked simple décor—brass and wood were his materials of choice. He did not allow plastic in the house, calling it ugly. Instead, he chose *au naturel*, the style of Heidi's current house in Pemba, Mozambique.

Heidi's father, Jim, came from Michigan and her mother, Glenetta, also known as Netta, was from Southern California. They met while sailing after Jim's graduation from Stanford University. When they met, Netta was engaged to another man; Netta's friend came running to her one day saying, "I met the perfect man for you."

"I'm engaged," Netta said, twirling a piece of her long blonde hair around her finger.

Her friend replied, "Oh, I know, but he's nothing compared to this guy."

Netta met Jim in a group setting, and they spent the whole evening talking to each other about their dreams. When they were in the car saying good-bye, Jim started to kiss Netta. Startled, she said she was spoken for.

"Oh well, it's just a little kiss; it's okay," he replied. After they were married, it became the family joke.

Netta and Jim wanted children, but for years they were unable to have them. Netta knew a young woman whose roommate became pregnant, and the girl, who had decided to give the baby up for adoption, moved in with Netta's parents. During this time Netta and Jim decided to adopt the baby. Even when the baby boy, named Zachary, was born with medical complications and doctors advised against the adoption, Netta and Jim's decision didn't change.

"Of course, we'll take him. We said we'd take him before he was born; he's ours. We won't not take him just because he has a defect," Netta told the doctor.

Shortly after adopting Zachary, Netta herself was suddenly pregnant. Heidi was born in August 1959; she was her parents' miracle baby. Less than a year later Heidi's younger sister, Diane, was born. Netta and Jim now had three children under three years old.

Though adopted, Zachary looked just like Heidi and Diane; he was a small towheaded child with light eyes. Heidi remembers flying kites with him. Like any child's early memories, they are full of jagged, colorful images: sand and surf, bright triangles in the deep blue sky, and a small boy running barefoot through the hot sand.

Unfortunately the play times with Zachary didn't last. When Zachary Baker was four and a half, he died from the complications in his intestines. Netta and Jim were heartsick at the death of their eldest child. Netta had difficulty coping and found it hard to speak about him even decades later. The girls missed their brother, but they were both so young. Netta told them, "Zachy's gone to heaven."

Almost a year after Zach's death, illness struck the family again; this time Heidi became ill with chicken pox and encephalitis, a sort of inflammation of the brain. She was packed in ice for two weeks. While Heidi was hallucinating in the hospital, Netta couldn't go in to be with her because it was contagious.

"It tore me up," Netta said, choking up at the memory. "I told God that if He would save her life and not let this child die, Heidi was entirely His to do with as He saw fit. And I guess He took me at my word. I did not tell Heidi I had done that. That was just between God and myself. I didn't tell her that until she was in her forties because I didn't want her to grow up thinking she was destined for anything...she never aimed for that kind of thing," Netta said, thinking back.

Netta was an opera singer. Heidi remembers watching her mother perform on stage in Los Angeles. From the time Heidi was three, they would journey into the city, excited to see their mother dressed in costume and to hear the deep, strong notes of her mezzo voice drifting to their ears from the stage. Netta loved sneaking a glance out at the audience, knowing that Jimmy and her two girls had gotten there early to get a good seat. She knew the girls would be sound asleep on their father's lap by intermission.

Heidi's father, Jim, was a businessman and an artist. Jim was a gentle and kind man; Heidi remembers him for his playfulness and how he tussled and tumbled with her on the floor when she was young. He also told the best bedtime stories, and each night, he either read or created his own wonderful, enchanted tale.

Heidi remembers his story, *The Tales of the Feathery Feather*. Each night the wind carried the feathery feather to a foreign land where it had marvelous adventures in the new place; sometimes it had trouble escaping from a particular sticky situation, and they'd listen intently, trying hard not to fall asleep before the end of their father's story, captivated by the new adventure.

Jim was an encourager at heart, and he told Heidi over and over again, emphatically, "You can do anything, darling."

Though she really wanted to believe him, Heidi doubted herself because she had dyslexia, causing tremendous difficulty in school. The teachers knew she was a bright child, but they didn't know what to do with her and her dyslexia. With crayons Netta taught Heidi to trace letters onto sandpaper, so that Heidi could feel the direction of the letters. Still, Heidi felt awkward and stupid.

"You are *not* stupid," her father told her. She looked up into his blue-green eyes, wanting to believe him.

Because of Heidi's struggles in school her parents decided to have a reading specialist test her. The professor who was testing Heidi kept Netta and Jim in the room while Heidi almost automatically solved the puzzles. The specialist then told Heidi they were going to test her to see how fast she could accomplish the tasks. Over and over again the woman made the small girl do the tasks as fast as she possibly could; this went on until Netta felt like screaming and Jim was ready to walk out. They hated to see Heidi straining under the demanding woman. When the tests concluded, Netta and Jim were both angry.

The reading specialist asked them if they had any questions.

"Yes," Netta said, "Why did you make her do that over and over again?"

"I did that on purpose," the woman responded, "so you would experience why this child can never have any pressure. Do not push this child. She tested at the genius level."

Netta and Jim had seen what pressure looked like, and they determined to let Heidi learn at her own pace and to help her all they could. In the end Heidi pressured herself because she wanted to excel. "I don't want to stay in this dummy class," she said, referring to a special reading class.

In the midst of her struggles Heidi took refuge in her animals to gain comfort, singing and rocking all twenty-two of them in her arms: dogs, cats, lizards, snakes, toads, birds, guinea pigs, hamsters, and frogs lived in her family home in Laguna Beach. At ten she planned to be a veterinarian when she grew up.

One day her father came into her room; he was crying. "Honey, I'm so sorry."

"Daddy, what's wrong?"

He embraced her in a bear hug. "I'm so sorry. I squished your toad in the door."

Heidi remembers it fondly: "How many people cry over a squished toad?" she asks smiling.

As a teenager Heidi bodysurfed and board-surfed. There's a picture of sixteen-year-old Heidi on the beach holding a surf board, standing straight as the board and slender in her bikini next to a cute blond surfer boy with long hair. Another photo shows her in action: her wet suit sleek and shiny as she balances expertly on the board, one knee up, about to stand. On her face she has the same focused look of determination that she wears in Mozambique.

Heidi's family vacationed near the water at a leisure ranch in Baja, Mexico, where the girls had plenty of beach time. Heidi and her family shared a ranch in Mexico with seventeen other families, and in the evenings they sat outside under the night sky and enjoyed intellectual conversation. Many of the co-owners of the ranch were professors from the University of California.

On their way to or from the ranch, even when Heidi was very young, they would stop in Tijuana at the garbage dump to bring food and clothing to the people living there. "Always respect the culture," Heidi's mother told the girls as they picked their way through the garbage. Netta spoke to the people in Spanish, and Heidi was drawn to the children who lived in the dump; some were the same age as Heidi. She remembers thinking that she wanted to help them and that they just looked like they needed love.

As a child Heidi experienced a variety of religious backgrounds. Her father was a nonpracticing Catholic, and her mother attended an Episcopalian church and sometimes took Heidi and Diane along. Heidi found that she actually enjoyed the services.

When Heidi was twelve or thirteen, a strange thing happened to her. At the girls' confirmation and first Holy Communion, the priest gingerly placed the small white wafer on Heidi's tongue, and as soon as she drank from the cup, she fell over backward, something known by Pentecostals as being slain in the Spirit. Heidi didn't know what had happened except that she was overwhelmed by the thought and feeling of God. Her parents and godparents thought she had merely fainted and carried her out of the church into the sunshine for fresh air. The surprised priest, a small, balding man with a round, pleasant face, said, "I've read about this. It happens when people are overcome by emotion."

Shortly after this, when Heidi was fourteen, her parents sent her to Switzerland for a year to study ballet. Six times a week, at least three hours a day, she studied with a ballet company in Lucerne, Switzerland. She stayed with family friends, who treated her as one of their own daughters. At the end of the year the company invited her to stay on to study ballet and become part of the company, but when her exchange program ended, she decided to return to her family in Laguna Beach.

The transition back to normal life was difficult, and after living cross-culturally, Heidi now found life in California a bit superficial. Her sophomore year of high school was different from her middle school years. Maybe she had outgrown normal adolescent awkwardness, or maybe she had acquired a sophistication from living abroad, but she suddenly found herself in the most popular group at school.

"Why is this, and why wasn't it before?" she asked herself, wondering why she had been chosen to be part of the in crowd. While some of it had its charms, like her first boyfriend, who was homecoming king, other things just seemed frivolous. Heidi wanted a broader experience after living in Switzerland. *I've got to find out how to look at people from the inside*, she thought.

With this in mind Heidi applied to be an American Field Service (now AFS-USA) student at a Native American reservation in central Mississippi. She spent her junior year there living among people who were certainly different from the people in Laguna Beach. Mississippi was southern in every way. Switzerland had broadened her culturally, but Mississippi was almost more foreign than another country.

Heidi lived in a dorm with Native American girls. At night, as she lay trying to fall asleep in her bunk bed, she would try to ignore the dull thumps of the things her roommates threw at her. Sometimes it was food, sometimes cockroaches.

"They hated me because I was white," Heidi recalled. Though rejection was painful and she cried often, Heidi was determined to make friends and determined to stay.

After a few months another AFS student invited Heidi to a revival on the Native American reservation. There were three white AFS students and about five hundred Native Americans at the revival. The preacher was dressed in full Native American regalia with a headdress and everything. Having been raised as a sort of bohemian intellectual, Heidi was intrigued and knew this was a true cultural experience.

Then the man began speaking of his hatred for white people, and Heidi wanted to hide and shrink down in her chair at the back of the basic cement building. She knew hiding was impossible, though; she was sopping wet from a spring thunderstorm, and her long blonde hair was dripping down her back. She found minimal comfort in noticing the woman playing the organ was white; at least she wasn't the only one people would stare at as the preacher told of the offenses he once held against white people.

Then he shifted in tone as he began to talk about his transformation; something had changed him and so filled him with love that he had found what it meant to love people from the inside. She found herself intensely intrigued by what he was sharing. This was why she was here; she was looking for a way to see people from the inside, to know them and love them that way.

As the Native American preacher spoke of his transformation, the hatred replaced by love, Heidi knew she wanted what he was offering. She wanted it badly enough she did not care what people thought of her when she responded to his invitation to come forward to meet the person who had transformed his life and the way he viewed people. In wet clothes and with dripping hair she ran to the front. Kneeling, she prayed, "Forgive me, Jesus. I'm a sinner." Tears leaked from her eyes; Heidi was desperate to find what the Native American man had found.

"You don't need to cry; it's OK," he told her. She was the only one who had responded to his invitation to come forward to meet Jesus.

"Calm down; you don't need to cry," someone else repeated.

"Yes, I do," she wailed, her heart breaking and her hands lifted in surrender. She didn't know the proper protocol, and she didn't care.

Many years later, after introducing many people to Jesus, Heidi laughed when remembering this moment: "The preacher thought he had a bummer night because I was the only one who responded to the altar call."

The next day Heidi awoke to the beauty of the morning—the sounds of singing, the brilliant blue of the sky, and the apple green grass. It was as if the outer world were a mirror of her inner state. The smells of warm earth and bonfire smoke drifted up through her window. The day was beautiful enough to remember forever: March 13, 1976.

That night she was supposed to go to a movie with friends, but Glenda, the white woman who had been playing the organ at the revival the night before, had invited her to another church meeting, telling Heidi, "You need the Holy Ghost."

Heidi remembered praying, "Father, Son, and Holy Ghost" in the Episcopalian church, so she thought, *I must need the Holy Ghost.*

Heidi chose to go with Glenda instead of going with her friends to the cinema, but little did she know that she opted for the much more engaging experience. The people were all white and all very odd compared to those at the meeting the night before. The women had high, beehive hairdos sprayed until the hair was absolutely stiff and sticking straight up in the air. The men all had short hair, which was odd for the mid-seventies era of the Rolling Stones, polyester, and long hair. Every woman dressed ultra-conservatively and wore a long skirt. The church was a Pentecostal Holiness Church.

Once again Heidi was an easy target. The night before she had been one of the only white people, and that night she was the only woman wearing jeans and mascara. The thirty people in attendance stared at the flower-child teenager in her tight brown jeans and short shirt. They hadn't had any new people among them in a long time. The pastor preached at Heidi.

"You have to be filled with the Holy Ghost," he said as he jumped over chairs. He sang, he danced, he clapped, he yelled, he banged a tambourine.

Either this is the happiest man I've ever seen, or this man is a hypocrite, Heidi thought. The church was full of energy and the people full of joy even though they looked so different from anything she'd experienced in the Catholic church in Switzerland or the small Episcopalian church of her child-hood, though she had loved each church experience for its own character. "What is this?" she wondered.

Then the pastor gave the invitation: "Who wants the Holy Ghost?!" They all turned and looked at Heidi.

Her heart was pounding. She felt like someone was tugging at the front of her shirt, and when she went to the front to kneel down, the entire church laid their hands on her while everything became very dark.

"Fill her with the Holy Ghost," they said.

Her eyes were closed in the darkest blackness she'd ever seen, and then she saw light exploding, and a language she didn't understand came pouring out of her mouth. As she shook and laughed and cried, she did not understand what was happening. Whatever it was, it was full of joy, and she got up eventually to dance. It was how she expressed herself, so maybe she did fit in with these people, the ones who were known as Holy Rollers for dancing in the aisles.

She didn't want to speak in English; she couldn't actually, for a short time. She could only speak this new foreign language of joy. Much later she would write a dissertation for her

PhD in systematic theology on glossolalia, the academic term for what is commonly known as speaking in tongues.

"You need to get baptized," someone said, and right there they rolled out a rusty bathtub, gave her a white dress to put on, and down into the water she went.

Soon Heidi began attending nightly meetings and spending weekends with the pastor and his wife. Another evening in church she felt so overshadowed by the Holy Ghost that she was not aware of anything else around her. While the church hooted and hollered, as loud as they always were, Heidi sat on the floor, her hands lifted. She couldn't even hear the thumping of the drum sets, one on each side of her.

She was having a vision, the first of many to come. Jesus was there with her, kissing her hand, her ring finger, and it felt as if oil was running down her arm, as he said, "You're my beloved, my bride, married to me." He spoke to her about being a missionary and minister, about how she would go to England, Africa, and Asia.

Though she had never heard a woman preacher, she started preaching the next day, telling her Native American friends what had happened to her. For the next four years she would preach to Alzheimer's patients in nursing homes and to drug addicts on the street.

Heidi was thrilled that she was experiencing and learning about real love and how to see others from the inside, but her new life did not come without sacrifices. Previously when Heidi had envisioned her future, she saw herself as a prima ballerina. But the life she thought might be filled with dance and ballet suddenly was not.

Heidi experienced the presence of God at the Pentecostal Holiness Church. When she spoke to Him and He spoke back, she felt his love, like something weighty and wonderful that moved through her veins. She wanted to lay down and soak it in. But a few days after Heidi started attending the Pentecostal Holiness Church, they gave her a list of rules. The church culture was so very different from what she had experienced in God's presence. The first thing the Pentecostal Holiness Church said: "Dance is a sin, and you can't do it."

"OK, that's fine," she said, tender enough to believe anything, to accept it all. They went far beyond dance—there were even rules about dress and makeup. When the church told her it was a sin to wear pants and that she had to wear skirts instead, she cut her jeans and sewed material into them because no one said they couldn't be jean skirts. She thought it must just be a part of knowing God, unaware at the time that rules and love were polar opposites. With her long, curly blonde hair, often with fresh flowers in it, and her cute clothes the church didn't believe she could be a hippie flower child who danced and loved Jesus. According to them one could dance only when filled with the Holy Ghost, or as Heidi calls it, doing the Holy Ghost two-step.

Giving up dance hurt. Sometimes Heidi could feel the ache for beauty in her bones; she had danced for hours every day, at least six days a week, for years. She also missed the art, the music, the culture.

She felt like she had fallen in love with a man so mysterious who came to her only in dreams and visions but who felt incredibly close to her. This dulled the sharp pain of giving up dance. She had traded one passion for another, and though she grieved deeply, this felt more satisfying. It was the hardest thing she had ever done.

Later in her life—after studying systematic theology, the study of theological truth, which had little to do with outward things and much to do with inward motives and theological thinking—she would discover the difference between the church, which was made up of fallen human beings, and Jesus, a perfect divine human being who not only went to weddings but who also made wine, and who probably danced.

Heidi's family and friends back in Laguna Beach were in for quite a surprise when she returned. It is easy to imagine why her parents thought she had joined a cult. Her friends left her because she was so different from who she was before she went to Mississippi, but she was still the same fun-loving girl. With her hand-sewn jean skirts Heidi was still a hippie teenager, but in Laguna Beach they just thought she was odd.

"When she left California for the reservation, Heidi had been a robust, fun-loving teenager, who was interested in dance and everything life had to offer. When she came back, she was quite pale, wan, wearing no makeup and old woman's clothes," Netta said about Heidi's return, assuming it was the women of the church who had sewn Heidi's Levi's into long skirts. "She came back saying 'Praise the Lord' every two minutes," Netta recalled with a laugh.

Heidi had been modeling since she was young. Before she left for Mississippi, she had been working with a well-known photographer who displayed his work in art exhibits and magazines. He was hosting a welcome home party for her and was there to meet her as she got off the plane. They were all shocked at the dramatic difference: a long skirt, a shirt that reached to her elbows, and a lack of makeup. Still, she was offered a modeling contract with Forbes Modeling Agency in New York City, but she knew she couldn't accept it because she had been told that "wealth gained by vanity will be diminished." She left for Mississippi as a dancer and a model and returned as a Pentecostal Holiness girl.

Heidi's parents, who have both now passed away, thought their daughter was dead. Of course, she was; she understood it to be the true call of Christianity—a laid-down life. Jesus said, "If anyone comes to Me and does not hate [her] father and mother...even [her] own life, [she] cannot be My disciple. And whoever does not bear [her] cross and follow Me cannot be My disciple."[1] The rules the church had laid out before her were certainly a heavy load to bear, but they were not necessarily the cross Jesus had been speaking about.

Heidi had to mark out a new life for herself in Laguna Beach. Her mother asked her to attend the Episcopalian church again, and she agreed, but Heidi was looking for something that felt more like the church in Mississippi. A girl Heidi knew told her about a neighbor who "spoke in tongues," and Heidi called him up on the telephone to interview him about his church.

"Do the women wear pants?" she asked suspiciously.

"Well, you know, they wear dresses a lot," he replied.

She visited, and though the women wore pants and makeup, she found a home among them in the small, beautiful chapel in Dana Point.

Chapter 6

SECOND LOVE

NOT VERY LONG after she returned from Mississippi, Heidi met a young man and the two started dating. He was older than she was, and Heidi was attracted to his maturity and intelligence. He was her first love, and she adored him, so she was thrilled when he asked her to marry him.

Heidi was preparing to send out the invitations for their wedding when she began to feel uneasy. Her fiancé loved God and was receptive when she told him about her experiences in Mississippi. When she told him about her vision to minister in Asia, England, and Africa, he told her he'd follow her anywhere.

But Heidi wanted to preach in Europe that summer, and she wasn't sure how it would work since they were getting married. She believed her fiancé when he said he'd follow her, but she wanted someone who had the same calling to be a missionary, not someone who would go into foreign ministry just for her. So she decided to pray and fast to know God's will.

She was in her sophomore year of college at Vanguard University. In charge of the campus ministries, Heidi hosted the visiting speakers and guest lecturers. Heidi was excited when a female minister came to speak to the campus; she was the only woman Heidi had ever heard preach, and Heidi was glad for the opportunity to have lunch with her afterward. When she told the woman she was not only getting married but she also wanted to minister in Europe, the woman questioned her about the upcoming marriage and said something like, "Doesn't sound like God to me."

Heidi had been praying and asking God for direction, so she took this as an answer. As soon as they were finished with lunch in the college cafeteria, Heidi ran into the prayer chapel, a small room where she had spent hours alone praying by herself. Sobbing, she threw herself prostrate on the floor.

"Jesus, I love you more than life, more than anything, more than him...." She pulled the engagement ring off of her finger and laid it down in front of her, as if at the feet of Jesus. "I give him to You." She cried there for hours; she didn't know how she would get up off of that floor. She didn't know how she would tell her fiancé the engagement was off.

Knocking on the door of his apartment, she waited there anxiously. "I love you, but God told me I can't marry you," she told him as they held each other. She tried to comfort him as he cried in her arms, but she also needed comfort. He was the one who had always been able to comfort her, but this time she couldn't let him.

He didn't understand; of course he didn't. She can remember few times in those months when she wasn't crying. "I loved him so much, oh my gosh," she told me, remembering the nineteen-year-old breathless girl with the broken heart.

In November, almost nine months later, Heidi went with her church on a skiing outing, and a man named Rolland Baker, son of famous missionaries to Asia, happened to sit beside her. She didn't know Rolland at all, so they just chatted informally as they drove to the ski resort in Mammoth Lakes from Southern California. Heidi told him about Asia, England, and Africa, and, intrigued, he managed a weak, "That's great."

He told her then about his growing-up-years in China as the son of missionary parents. That's when Heidi realized that Rolland's mother had been her sixth-grade teacher when his family was on sabbatical in the United States that year. As a child Heidi loved hearing her teacher's missionary stories.

What a coincidence that she knew Rolland's mother! This was a moment of real connection for Heidi and Rolland, but because Rolland was a decade or so older than her, Heidi did not think about him in a romantic kind of way.

When she tells the story of how she met Rolland, Heidi often says, "Out to lunch once, and then we were married. I was on a plane to Indonesia with a man I didn't know, a one-way ticket, and thirty dollars."

Though Heidi remembers the brevity of their early relationship, Rolland remembers visiting Heidi at her house. He remembers enjoying that they talked only about God rather than going out to see a movie or playing volleyball on the beach. Heidi was quite content just to talk, and Rolland remembers finding her singing to God in her room on Saturday mornings. He liked that she was different than all the other girls he knew.

A few months after they met on the ski trip, Heidi spent Christmas at her parent's ranch on the tip of Baja and then went on to Mexico City to do some short-term work in the slums with the poor. One evening, as she spent time in prayer, she received direction for her future. She felt God told her she would be ordained before she was twenty-one; this was at a time when women were not ordained as ministers. She would also finish her degree in her third year at Vanguard University. Additionally she would go to Indonesia as a missionary and preach with Mel Tari, a well-known itinerant preacher from Indonesia, and she would marry Rolland Baker.

Hearing the name Rolland Baker was shocking; she hardly knew him!

The day Heidi was supposed to leave Mexico City to return to California, some of the children who lived next door to where she was staying in the slums were playing with her passport, and unbeknownst to her, her visa had fallen out of it. When she got to the airport, she was unable to leave the country, and she returned to her tiny room to search for the visa. In the mail that same day, the day she was supposed to be on the flight back to California, she received seven long letters from Rolland Baker. "Mushy, mushy," she said when she described them to me, but they confirmed to her that yes, indeed, she was supposed to marry Rolland.

When Heidi got home from Mexico City, Rolland came directly to her university. He sat with her often in her small office, while she, the hippie flower child, made herbal tea. She loved drinking herbal tea and offered him some.

"Would you like some herb tea?" she asked.

"Oh, yes, thank you," he replied, drinking herb tea every time he came to her office.

After he married Heidi, Rolland told her the truth. He hated herbal tea. He said, "That is the most disgusting stuff. I can't believe anyone would ever think of drinking that stuff; it tastes like medicine."

"Sweetie, why did you drink it?" she asked him.

"I loved you so much I drank it and could hardly taste it," he told her.

Though Heidi and Rolland's relationship was progressing, not everyone was on board with it. When Heidi's father met Rolland for the first time, he said, "So what do you do, save souls?" He was politely hostile. Her parents couldn't understand people taking religion so seriously. They had wanted Heidi to go to New York to be a prima ballerina, or at least to attend an Ivy League school. Instead, she was attending a college with an Assemblies of God affiliation and planning to be a missionary. It seemed to them that she was throwing her life away.

Still, this didn't slow Heidi and Rolland's relationship. Heidi had been in Mexico City in January, and by May, after one lunch at a Chinese restaurant (with Rolland making sure she liked Chinese food) and one dinner, they were married. The ceremony was held on the beach in front of Heidi's house.

Turns out that the Indonesian preacher Heidi heard about in her vision was Rolland's best friend who invited them to speak at a conference with him in June, so they planned to leave for Indonesia in the beginning of June, just two weeks after their wedding. For their wedding they asked for no gifts, just money for their airfare.

For their honeymoon, before the trip to Indonesia, Rolland's best man booked them a honeymoon suite on the Queen Mary. They took the ferry, standing among the crowds of people; it was Memorial Day weekend. When they arrived at the boat, the receptionist looked at the newly married couple: "I'm sorry, but there's been a mistake. Your room isn't available. There's nothing we can do." Heidi and Rolland sat down outside on the curb with their luggage.

"It was our first day of married life, and we sat there on the curb with nowhere to go, as we often did later on mission trips," Rolland remembered. They asked the receptionist if they could borrow the phone book, so they could look for a hotel. They chose one at random and prayed there was a room available. The receptionist who answered their call said, "We are completely booked, but we do have a room available for you. I don't know what happened, but the gentleman who had the room had to leave suddenly."

When they got to their hotel room, the first thing they did was count the money they had received as wedding gifts. They were thrilled to find they had almost enough for two one-way plane tickets to Asia. They counted out almost $1,200; one-way tickets were $800 each.

Still needing at least $400, they were quite pleased when

Rolland's friend called to say he needed a photographer for the crusade. If Rolland, who was a photographer, would do the job, he would pay them $500. In the two weeks they had before they left for Indonesia, they had to set everything in order. Rolland had to sell his sporty silver Mazda and give up his apartment. Each day they had a long list of things that needed to be done so that the next day they could accomplish the things on the next list. It was intense pressure, and it certainly was not the idyllic first few weeks of marriage.

Heidi's parents thought they were being irresponsible and downright unprepared, but Heidi was twenty years old and had married a man twelve years older. They were still disappointed that it didn't work between Heidi and her former fiancé, but they didn't know that in the future she would receive something even better, the kingdom manifesting through her partnership with Rolland.

As the plane lifted off from LAX, Heidi and Rolland leaned their heads back in their small, economy-class seats, exhausted and excited. Leaving was their first victory—and it was a huge one. They didn't know where they were going to live or what they were going to do, but they were going. Heidi and Rolland would not return to live in America for any length of time but would make their home in foreign lands—Asia, England, and Africa—for love, for which they would go anywhere and do anything.

Chapter 7

THE BEGINNING OF
MISSIONARY LIFE

HEN THEY ARRIVED in Asia, Rolland and Heidi were desperately poor. No one knew, and they would never tell anyone. After they bought their one-way plane tickets, they had thirty dollars left from their wedding money. As they drove down the main street of Jakarta, Indonesia, friends of theirs pointed out the American Express offices where they could cash their traveler's checks. Heidi and Rolland were too embarrassed to tell them they didn't have any traveler's checks. When they visited a church as guest speakers, the pastor handed them money for a taxi, not knowing it was all they would have for food, transportation, and everything else they might need.

When the stadium meeting in Jakarta was over, Rolland's friend was on his way back to his home on the island of East Timor, where there was a huge revival. He bought Heidi and Rolland tickets to Bali, where they could stay with his friends who ran a children's center and worked as missionaries. In Bali, Heidi and Rolland were slightly overwhelmed by the faces of homemade gods with candles glowing behind their eyes, incense in the air as heavy as sweet perfume, and altars for the sacrifices to the many Hindu representations of god. In the end these things only made them more sure that Bali was the right place for them to start their work. It was an island of three million people with only two or three Christian missionaries. When they looked into the history of Bali, they found that it was a country that had been closed to missionaries for many years.

Two hundred years earlier, when the first Christian missionary arrived on the island, there were severe clashes with Hindus. The first Balinese Christian convert, who was called Nicodemus, became a student of the missionary who converted him. But Nicodemus's family disowned him. The missionary strongly encouraged Nicodemus to baptize others, but the pressure against Nicodemus from his former community was so intense that eventually he killed his teacher the missionary, renounced his faith, and returned to his former community to be executed according to Balinese law. It was sometime afterward that the law closed missionaries out of Bali completely. When the island opened again it was under strict control and in a spirit of hostility. Converted Christians were ostracized and thrown out of villages. They had to move across the island to their own villages. For years the country of Holland, where the first missionary came from, discouraged any missionary activity.

When Heidi and Rolland arrived in the center where they would be staying, they met the couple they would be serving alongside. The woman took them on a short tour of the center, and when she opened the door to the room where Heidi and Rolland would be staying, there happened to an enormous iguana on their bed; it was so big it took up half of the double bed. The woman apologized and shooed it away, but when they walked into the bathroom, they found a scorpion in their bathtub. It was a rough start.

Soon after they arrived, Heidi and Rolland caught a taxi to one of the few Christian churches on the island, where they were scheduled to speak. When they told the driver that he was taking them to a church, the driver stopped abruptly and furiously ordered them out of the car. He threw the money they gave him onto the street and drove off in a rage. It was difficult to make an inroad with the people, who routinely went to witch doctors to curse white tourists in order to get more money out of them.

But Rolland and Heidi had no money. Their home church had committed to give them a thousand dollars a month, but their bank account was still empty. They stood in line at the phone booth for hours to call the pastor to find out why they hadn't received anything yet; finally they got to use the phone. Shouting loudly into the plastic mouthpiece, they reached the pastor of their home church: "Hi. We're calling from Bali. Have you been able to put anything into our account?"

"Nope, not a penny. How are you guys?"

The pastor had gotten into trouble and things in the congregation were not looking good, so the money never did come through. Rolland remembers not even having money to buy a Coca-Cola.

The people with whom they stayed gave them a meager breakfast every morning: fern shoots, papaya, and marmite, a concentrated yeast paste often served on toast or sandwiches. Once, when visitors from New Zealand came to the center and offered to take them for "tea," Heidi and Rolland were unaware that "tea" meant an evening meal that actually turned out to be a steak dinner. They couldn't believe it, and they tried not to look too excited. They hadn't eaten a real meal for months—not since they left California—and they were hungry. Heidi lost so much weight that her wedding ring fell off.

After many months in Bali they decided to go home. They were poor and perhaps somewhat discouraged. They had not really seen much happen, and they didn't have a way to reach the people. They were barely surviving themselves. Having little money, they went to Singapore Airlines because someone told them the airline gave discounts to missionaries. They got half price fares, which enabled them to get as far as Hawaii, where they stayed for a number of months, working with poor Hawaiians on the north shore of Oahu.

Heidi and Rolland worked with a pastor who was in the middle of a divorce and was happy to have company in his home and help at his small church. They settled in as co-pastors and wrote newsletters, typing them up on an electronic typewriter. People from home occasionally sent support, and they were able to purchase their first car, a station wagon that leaked oil and caught fire, so when they turned it off at night, they could see the flames licking up from underneath. They called it the Dragon Wagon. The tires were different sizes, the power steering didn't work, and there were holes in the floor from rust, but they didn't care; they were just excited to have a car.

Teenagers were a large part of the congregation, and most lived in sugar cane fields. They were ashamed to bring their parents to church because they didn't have nice clothes. These locals were not the most welcoming, either. Heidi and Rolland heard of a white visitor who had been slashed by razor blades as he walked through a sugar cane field. Despite the danger and the teenagers' reluctance to bring their families to church, Heidi and Rolland loved the people, the beauty of the sunsets over the water, the surfers riding the big, heavy waves, the daily rainbows, and the luaus. However, they didn't feel called to Hawaii for the rest of their lives. They saved enough money to return to California, and they arrived back in Laguna Beach many months after they first left for Indonesia.

After some time at home in California, the couple still felt they were called to the poor even though their first trip abroad hadn't been exactly what they expected. They decided to have more of a plan of how to reach people, and they thought that maybe if they used the creative arts they could reach people more effectively. They would use their passions—Rolland's photography and technical expertise and Heidi's dance (and love of art and culture)—in their missionary work.

When Heidi attended the Pentecostal Holiness Church at sixteen, she was told to give up dance, and the sacrifice had pricked her heart like a sharp needle. But a few years later, as she was praying one day, she saw someone dancing with her; in her mind's eye she saw herself as a child with flowers in her long curly hair. The man in her vision was silhouetted as he picked her up and danced with her all around a field. He loved the dance as much as she did. They pirouetted. They leaped across the field. When the man smiled at her, she knew what her Father was trying to tell her: she was free to dance again. Heidi would take dance to Asia with a dance and drama team.

Before she married Rolland, Heidi had gone to the United Kingdom with a well-known missions organization called Youth With a Mission, (YWAM), where they had performed a dance drama called *Toymaker and Son*, an allegory about Jesus. Heidi came to life as a beautiful ballerina, spinning and pirouetting across the street, where they performed, groups of people admiring her agility and grace.

Heidi and Rolland wanted to use the same drama in Asia. Normally YWAM didn't release their material to outsiders, but they released it to Heidi, and the director even came to California to direct and train the group who planned to go to Asia with Heidi and Rolland to perform.

Heidi and Rolland gathered together a group of college-aged students for a six-month mission to Asia. Because of their previous experience in Indonesia Heidi and Rolland were cautious when they spoke to the students about the upcoming trip: they didn't know where they would stay or where they would visit, not to mention how they would get there. Once

again they had no money, but the fifteen college students who
had signed up to go with them were not deterred. When parents asked Rolland if it was safe for their children, he didn't
know how to answer them.

"I don't know. We're going to Red China," he replied, giving
them little confidence.

Some of the parents thought the team would never leave
the country, thinking they had seen this naive idealism before.
After pooling their resources, the team was still short $12,000.
It was a Saturday, and they were performing the dance drama
at the University of California, Irvine. They had until 1:00 p.m.
to confirm their tickets with Singapore Air, and it was 12:30
when they finished performing. They were idealistic, confident
that they were leaving for Asia even though they did not yet
have the funding; they had already gotten their vaccinations
and packed their suitcases.

Outside in the balmy California weather, Rolland waited
for Heidi to finish receiving applause and reassuring everyone
that yes, everything would fall into place. It was ten minutes
before 1:00 p.m. when a silver Rolls-Royce pulled up alongside
the curb where Rolland stood. The driver of the car, dressed in
a three-piece suit, smiled at Rolland and introduced himself.

"How's your faith?" he asked Rolland, as he handed him an
envelope.

"Fine, just fine," Rolland said.

The man had seen a rehearsal of the *Toymaker and Son* they
had done in Laguna Beach, and he wanted to help. Inside the
envelope was a deposit slip for exactly $12,000.

They saw so many miracles on that trip to Asia. They were
under intense pressure and found it extremely stressful trying
to lead fifteen others when they didn't know what they were
doing or where they were going. Rolland prayed he'd never
have to go through this again, but in retrospect, without that

kind of stress, he didn't think they would have seen the types of miracles they saw. There was something about desperation, and they were certainly desperate. Rolland laughs at the thought of fellow ministers and missionaries he knows now who advertise their mission trips as if they were something like parades: "Come see miracles, the power of God. It will change your life, and you'll never be the same."

Everyone on the team remembered one miracle particularly. They were staying in a village in the Philippines in the small house of one of the villagers. They slept on the cement floor and tried to protect themselves from the spiders that dropped down from the ceiling. One day a member of their dance drama team fell down concrete steps on her way outside to the bathroom, and she lay in pain at the bottom of the stairs unable to move; it seemed as if she had broken her back. She screamed for help.

The team's first response was to pray—they hadn't had money for a hotel room, and they certainly didn't have money for a hospital visit. As the team prayed for her, something like fire burned through her back, a sensation that moved up and down, and then the pain was gone. Heidi told the woman she had to get up and walk, that she needed to exercise her faith. The young woman had previously complained she had never seen a real miracle, but she got up and walked nevertheless, and the pain really was gone.

After this experience Rolland couldn't believe they had actually invited people to go with them on this trip. It taught him the real dangers inherent in their travel. Meanwhile, the team was having difficulty doing the dance dramas well. Rolland was trying to run the sound system off inverted batteries because there was no electricity, but the sound was so weak that no one could hear much of anything and the sound they did hear was really distorted. There was bird poop all over the stages they used. And it was swelteringly hot; the people were constantly wiping sweat from their brows because of the humidity. Still, people responded. Whole crowds were impacted by their message of God's love. They saw people "getting saved en masse," and they thought they were pleasing God because this is what the church had taught them to do— to evangelize huge crowds and move on.

They ended their time in the Philippines at a Bible school in a small village. It was an old, broken-down place that had been run-down since World War II. At the school there was a hunk of a bus worse than the Dragon Wagon, and they took the team all over the village in it. Heidi and Rolland felt so sorry for the students at the Bible school that they gave them all of their team's remaining money to fix the bus.

Heidi and Rolland didn't tell their team that they had no way to get from the village back to Manila. When they were having breakfast on their last day in the village and everyone was preparing to leave, Heidi and Rolland were the only ones who knew they couldn't actually leave.

During breakfast two Filipino men in uniform showed up saying that when they were ready, the plane was waiting. The general of the Filipino army had sent his private plane to retrieve them at their last stop. Heidi and Rolland looked at each other and smiled, sharing a sigh of relief. As they sat in the lounge of the plane, sinking back into the seats, they watched the runway overgrown with weeds move away from them as they took off. They were the only plane in sight.

They returned to California tired but much more satisfied than they had been on their first trip to Asia, and they decided to return a third time. This time they knew what to expect. Heidi prepared her own play, and Rolland took a projector and a screen and did lap dissolve slides, a new technique that allowed the end of one scene to overlap the beginning of the next scene by fading out the former while fading in the latter. Even in the sugar-cane plantations of the Philippines, they used floodlights and an intricate multi-track recorder.

They had decided to return to the Philippines where they were so warmly welcomed previously. A different sort of experience awaited them, however. They were embraced warmly and found themselves staying with the wealthiest family in Bacolod City in the province of Negros Occidental. Bacolod City was extremely poor at the time. The dictator, Marcos, had monopolized the sugar cane economy, and corruption under his rule crippled the entire country's economy.

During their visit a hurricane was raging, and as a result the weather was miserable. The rain kept coming, turning everything into mud. The huge house at which they were staying had a wrought iron gate where kids congregated, begging for help. Each time Rolland and Heidi left the house, they would pass right by these children, most of them orphaned or abandoned. As the rain continued, the situation grew worse: the kids wandered aimlessly through the streets in the rain, plodding through the mud that came up to their small calves. Many of them were sick with parasites and tuberculosis, and the ones who had tuberculosis were coughing up blood.

When the kids watched them come and go in their fancy car, Heidi felt a pang of guilt. When they left the dry car for the comfort of the warm house, running through the rain, a few of the children called to them for help. One of the girls wore nothing but rags that were falling off her too-thin body; tears were running down her upturned face, her fingers wriggling through the bars, her arms reaching for them.

Heidi and Rolland felt they couldn't stand by and not do anything. Heidi went to the small girl and took her by the hand, leading her to the car and asking the chauffeur where they could find a new dress for her. They took her to the market; it was a little less crowded than usual with the hurricane's winds knocking items off shelves and blowing away anything that wasn't pinned down. They chose a pale yellow dress for her, and when they asked her if she liked it, she only stared at it with a faraway look in her eyes. This was probably her first shopping experience—her first new dress.

When they returned to the house, they took her inside and bathed her. Heidi noticed her ribs jutting out from underneath her skin, and she wished there was more they could do than merely buying her new clothes. Heidi lifted her out of the tub and dried her off with a fluffy towel, dressing her in the cute yellow dress. For the first time, the girl smiled at Heidi. When she wouldn't leave Heidi's side, pressing her face shyly into Heidi's hip, Heidi felt a motherly protectiveness toward the little one. Not yet sure how she could send her away on her own the same way the girl had come, Heidi led her into the kitchen to eat. She would think about it while the child had some dinner.

Their host came home while they were feeding her. Standing at the door, he let out a gasp of indignation.

"Don't you know their parents pay them to do that? It's a big ruse. You're not supposed to help people like that!"

Heidi and Rolland were devastated. They had seen something they hadn't seen before—real suffering—and they had met a need. It was different than what they had been doing, and it captured their hearts.

Rolland and Heidi knew they couldn't continue traveling with dance dramas and mere preaching-oriented productions, staying for three days just to say good-bye and leave. In the beggar children at the front gate and their rich hosts with whom they stayed, they had seen a picture of the rich and the poor.

The Bakers had wanted to reach thousands at a time and had succeeded. But there was something different about caring for the needs of the little girl at the gate that had captured their imaginations. It was something tangible, and they recalled Jesus's words that whatever they did for the least of these, they did for Him. It was like a secret of the kingdom had been unlocked in their hearts.

Heidi would again give up the dance, at least in the form of her dance dramas, which were partly fueled by their ambition to be successful. Success to them had looked like reaching the masses.

"Jesus healed the sick; He fed the people who were hungry. He cast out their demons; He didn't just host a large event. He didn't just count numbers. He cared for the actual person," Heidi told me. She was realizing she needed to do the same.

The little Filipino girl at the gate taught Heidi two things: she didn't know a thing and the poor would become her greatest teachers.

Chapter 8

TURNING POINT: ASIA 2.0

Not long after they returned from their short-term trip to the Philippines, Heidi and Rolland left for Asia full time. Two years later Heidi was pregnant. When she was seven-and-a-half months pregnant, they realized they would have to fly to Hawaii to have the baby because the church they had previously co-pastored had given them health insurance as a gift, but it was only valid in Hawaii. Though she was too far along in the pregnancy to fly, she got on the plane.

Months passed in Hawaii, with Heidi and Rolland adjusting to parenthood with their baby son they named Elisha. After Elisha was born, she and Rolland returned to the continental United States for a little over a year so Heidi could get her master's degree in missiology and Rolland could finish his bachelor's while earning a master's degree in theology at the same time.

In Heidi's postgraduate classes in missiology she read books and listened to mission theology that said, "Go through the struggles, the difficulties, with the people with whom you're working. If they don't have running water or electricity, neither do you. If they can't afford cheese, neither should you." Heidi and Rolland adopted this theology as their own.

When they finished their degrees, they moved back to Indonesia, the first nation they'd visited after they married, to live in the slums of Jakarta with the poor. Heidi and Rolland practiced voluntary poverty so they could use their resources to serve the poor. Their small family did not eat meat or cheese, and they lived without electricity and hot water. She remembers Elisha screaming as she poured cold water over him in the bathtub. "I thought no boundaries meant you were a stellar missionary," Heidi told me. "We didn't understand balance." Their ethos was to give everything without concern for their own needs, even if it meant deprivation.

In Jakarta their family lived all together in one room that was part of a concrete house called Shalom run by Christian missionaries in the Senin slums of Jakarta. While Rolland went off each day to teach English, Heidi spent her time sitting with the women in the dirty streets. Heidi, who had only two outfits and very little food, had given away everything else in Hawaii. (It was the first time she felt like she was supposed to give away all that she and Rolland owned, but it would not be the last time.)

The Indonesian women, with their silky black hair tied back into buns and early wrinkles in their faces from poverty, took care of Heidi. They gave her water, which commonly gave her dysentery, and they shared their food with her as she sat with them in front of their shacks made with corrugated iron roofs; a few of the women lived in huts made from cardboard boxes and small pieces of tin and garbage.

Through this process Heidi learned dependence. American culture had taught her that independence was to be prized, and that meant strength, self-reliance, hard work, and success. But she was realizing that what she really needed was dependence on God, someone far stronger and more able than she was. Heidi was discovering that as she became like a child, learned dependence, and allowed them—the poor—to provide for her, she was able to build real relationships with them. Healthy relationships were interdependent; she was not their savior—that was the old colonial mind-set. Heidi knew her new friends had so much to teach her.

Somewhere around this time Heidi felt that Jesus showed her that fruit would always come when she went to the poorest, loneliest, and most broken people. She was to find the hungriest, the sickest, the most needy and minister to them, because they're the ones who wanted more of God.

Heidi was determined to learn the language. Without the language she would not be able to go deeper in her friendships. She started a job program for the women, most of whom had never even heard of Jesus, teaching them to make greeting cards, while they taught her Bahasa Indonesia. She was fluent after a year and she made many friends in the process, hardly sleeping because socializing was such a large part of life in the slums. People would stay at her house until the early morning; she would sleep for just a few hours before she was awake with Elisha and off to sit with the women again. "My poor husband is not wired like I am, and he couldn't handle all of the people. I'm an introvert; he's an extreme introvert."

"You gave me the gift of your language. *Terima kasi*," she thanked them. She felt like the greatest gift she could give them was Jesus, and they said yes to Him. Soon they were praying together. They really were family, living in community, the candles flickering dimly as they laughed and talked into the early morning.

As Heidi went out each day, she always took Elisha with her; she walked so much that she wore out twelve or thirteen strollers on him. The women with whom she worked just loved Elisha, and one of Heidi's friends once gave him a baby duckling as a present. It was his first pet. It had soft yellow fur and chirped softly in his small hands. He loved to squeeze it close to his small body.

One day he came to Heidi, saying, "Mom, wake up my

duck." His chubby face gazed up at her as he tried to hold up the duckling's drooping head.

He had killed it.

"He's in heaven now, with Jesus, sweetie," she told him. Heidi's heart hurt for Elisha the way her father probably felt when he killed her toad in the door. It's hard to watch your child encounter suffering and death for the first time. At the same time Heidi was acutely aware that the children in the slums confronted suffering and death daily.

When her blond-haired Elisha was five, Heidi was pregnant again, and this time she was very sick. She wasn't sure why, and there was little medical care available. Then suddenly Heidi and Rolland's visas were revoked, and they had to leave Indonesia altogether. Heidi was crushed; she was finally fluent in the language, and Elisha was also speaking the language. She tried to hold back her tears on the plane.

They went to Hong Kong to stay with Rolland's parents, who were missionaries there. When they arrived and sought medical care for Heidi, the doctors told her that she would have died had they stayed in Indonesia. Heidi had toxemia, a condition often fatal for mother and child. She was malnourished from eating mainly bananas, rice, and fern shoots for four years. Her body was full of poison and severely swollen, and when touched, her skin dented in and stayed that way. Nevertheless, Crystalyn was born perfectly healthy, rating a ten on the scale the hospital used to rate the health of babies. Heidi had arrived in Hong Kong in a state of emergency, but after delivering her daughter, she slowly recovered.

Hong Kong was harsh and cold compared to Indonesia. The new family of four lived in the one of the most densely populated areas in the world. They lived in a thirty-story building with sixty-five thousand people in their apartment complex. It even had an underground shopping center, making it possible to never leave the apartment. People would work long hours seven days a week, leaving little time for family or anything else, and everyone was in a hurry, dashing like mad to and fro. The ones who weren't able to be productive were forgotten; old women were deserted, living on the street. "It was terrible on Heidi at first; she'd walk the streets crying," Rolland once said.

But Heidi was resilient, and she picked up where she left off in Indonesia. More than anything she was learning tenacity. She wouldn't stop; she wouldn't deny her calling. She tried to remember His goodness everyday no matter what the external circumstances felt like. Finding a park where the old women congregated, she sat with them each day, again forced to become childlike in order to learn their language, Cantonese. They were happy to teach her, but at first they didn't want her to speak about Christianity, of which they had never heard.

However, they did allow her to pray for them when they were sick. When they were healed there on the park benches, they wanted to know the man she prayed to named Jesus. The grannies had never experienced the sense of dignity they found in this love, so right there in the park they smashed the statues they once had worshipped. Heidi affectionately called the women who were healed the "granny church," and that's how they started their church in Hong Kong, The Home of Loving Believers, which was open around the clock every day of the week. There people were always able to find someone who would love them. Those who didn't have homes or who were addicted to drugs came to the church, and many gave up their drugs in exchange for this supernatural love that they first encountered through Heidi and Rolland.

Not long after they arrived in Hong Kong, Heidi decided to take the advice of an English missionary who had been working with the poor in Hong Kong for years. The missionary became a mentor to Heidi, and she taught her to live a life of sacrifice. Heidi had done it before; it would be fine to do it again.

Jackie Pullinger lived in the Walled City, a lawless area where even the police didn't dare venture and where the rats were the size of cats. The walls of the dwellings were covered with moss. Because Jackie was seeing incredible results—drug addicts getting free from their addictions and street sleepers finding homes and a new family—Heidi wanted to be like her and was willing to try to live the way she did for the sake of the poor, no matter how difficult it was. The Bakers moved to a one-room apartment on the ninth floor of a building without an elevator. Not even the poorest wanted to live in that dark, dirty room without kitchen plumbing or electrical wiring.

"We ate instant noodles. Elisha and Crystalyn learned how to cook noodles over a metal thing that sent out jolts of electricity," Heidi recounted to me. She didn't remember there being much play in their house. Every day they walked up and down the nine flights of steps, past prostitutes, and gangsters and through the sweet smell of incense to get to their apartment. Heidi seemed to be trying so hard to do missions the way others told her was the "right way."

It would have been too difficult for anyone and proved to be too difficult for Heidi, who collapsed on the street after three years in Hong Kong. Too weak to make it up the stairs to her apartment, she had to be helped into bed. Fever, dizziness, body aches: she thought it was the flu. When the pain wouldn't go away, she was diagnosed with a severe immune disorder. A week at a vacation island, Chung Jow Island, where Heidi went to rest, did not help her to recover, and she could do nothing but lie in bed in severe pain. Heidi was not used to being taken care of. She had always done the caring for, from 8:00 a.m. to 10:00 p.m., seven days a week.

Heidi was then diagnosed with myalgic encephalomyelitis, now sometimes known as chronic fatigue syndrome. Rolland told me, "It was very difficult to diagnose. Most people think it's in a patient's head, but it's actually a viral infection of the brain and spinal cord that affects the circulation and tightens up the nerves." Researchers are still studying the causes and symptoms of this disease, as well as the links between various viruses that affect the neurological system and chronic fatigue. There were no real treatments available for Heidi at the time.

Heidi needed to take time away from the mission field to recover, so she went to Alaska, where the woman she called her spiritual mother, Juanita Vincent, lived. Heidi met Juanita when she was a student at Vanguard University; at the time Juanita was one of the only female ministers Heidi had ever met, which encouraged Heidi that it was possible to be a minister and missionary even though she was a woman.

There in Fairbanks, Heidi spent four months in a dark room listening to the Bible on cassette. She was in so much pain she couldn't bear to look at light, so she closed the blinds on the windows. She was so weak that sometimes she had to crawl to the bathroom in the dark. She felt completely useless, and she missed her kids, who had stayed in Asia with Rolland.

"Don't feel sorry for me. This is the best time in my life because I feel so close to God," Heidi told Rolland over the phone.

"That's when she learned she was valuable to God even though she couldn't do anything," Rolland told me. This was a huge shift in orientation for Heidi. She would stop trying to live up to others' expectations and instead start living in response to this new intimacy with God she felt.

After four months Heidi got out of bed to attend a church service. Suddenly, in the middle of the service, she felt relief. For the first time in months she felt strong. The next day she even went for a walk in the woods. Gradually she was able to do things that she hadn't been able to do for a long time.

Shortly afterward, when praying about what she should do next and whether she should return to Asia, Heidi heard God tell her that it was time for her to go to England; it was time to get her PhD. She thought it odd that He would tell her to do this when she was not fully well, but stranger things had happened. She spoke with Rolland, and he agreed, which confirmed in her heart that this was the next step.

Chapter 9

ENGLAND

O N THE STREETS of London, with the towers of West-
minster Abbey jutting toward the gray English sky,
Heidi braced herself for another blow. A homeless woman, dressed in a men's suit and dress shoes, had just
kicked her hard in the leg.

When Heidi first approached the street woman, who was
sitting on the winter-cold sidewalk under a blanket, she
thought she was talking to a man. When the man grimaced,
revealing slightly uneven and yellowing teeth, and grumbled,
"Go away," Heidi realized the he was a she. With her brown
hair cropped close to her head and wearing men's clothing,
the woman showed no clear signs of her real gender.

Heidi ignored the comment completely and smiled at her,
as if the woman had not told her to go away. "What's your
name? Would you like a baked potato?"

Heidi handed the foil-wrapped potato to her, but the woman
swung violently at Heidi's hand, as if to block any contact
with another human being, even contact as small as a stranger
offering her food. As Heidi watched the potato roll out onto
the street, she felt a sharp pang of compassion for the woman
she learned was named Jen.

"Leave me alone, woman," Jen screamed. This was followed
by a string of expletives, and in a split second, before Heidi had
time to respond, Jen was up on her feet, squaring off against
Heidi, her men's dress shoes inches from Heidi's black English
boots. Jen's eyes narrowed into dark slits. She spit on Heidi.

At the same moment Heidi noticed Sean, her drunk Irish Catholic friend, standing off to the side, watching. Although Sean, also homeless, had said nothing to Heidi except a few expletives for the last year and a half, Heidi considered him a friend, always bringing him potatoes, baked beans, or sandwiches when she came into this section of town on her way to King's College, where she was studying for her PhD in systematic theology. Some days Sean was so drunk he didn't seem to recognize Heidi, and he threw the food on the ground, mumbling, his cheeks burning bright red.

"Look at me, woman," Jen demanded, taking Heidi's face in her dirty hand and pulling it away from the direction of Sean. "I will rip your face open, slit your throat, and throw you into the Thames," Jen said, her eyes darting to the piece of broken bottle lying a few yards away.

Heidi remained silent.

Instead of moving to pick up the glass, Jen, unable to look directly into Heidi's blue eyes, shoved Heidi's face away and punched her in the ribs. Heidi doubled over. Then Jen kicked her in the shins. Heidi finally cried out. She purposefully stared into Jen's eyes. "Jen, you can decide what you're going to do. You can slit my throat and throw me into the Thames, but I have to sit down because I'm just tired," Heidi said, her voice shaking. Heidi's body was weak from the chronic fatigue, and even though she believed in turning the other cheek, she didn't think she could stand any more physical pain.

Some days Heidi felt OK, but she couldn't run or play with her young children because of the illness. Although she was able to attend most of her classes, Heidi cried a lot and retreated to bed often. It was a long fight of faith for Heidi. They had tried everything—both traditional medical doctors and homeopathic physicians. Some days the pain was terrible, and Heidi never knew how long it would last. She felt like quitting every other day.

Today was one of those days. Standing on the banks of the Thames, Heidi tried to avoid thinking about how much she would rather just die than feel any more pain, but Heidi's plea seemed to make Jen angrier, and she began to punch her fists into Heidi's kidneys.

Just then Heidi heard a strong man's voice say, "Leave her alone, or I'm going to call the police."

Jen and Heidi looked to see who had interfered. Others had just walked by, most of them crossing to the other side of street when they saw the beating—it was common in England to avoid contact with strangers.

At the sound of the man's voice Heidi inwardly rejoiced, and she looked over at the man who was saving her from Jen. Sean?

"Thank you...Sean. Thank you," Heidi said, in barely more than a whisper. "But don't call the police. I love Jen, you know. She is going to know God's love."

Sean responded by mumbling his usual expletives, as he lifted Heidi into his arms, carrying her as he would a baby, taking her away from Jen.

Then Sean began to cry. For a moment he held Heidi silently as he tried to find his voice. Heidi noticed his face was redder than she had ever seen it, and he needed to clear his throat a few times before he could speak. Because he had never spoken to her, she didn't even know if he was in his right mind. She wondered at the fact that he was still holding her, but she would have rather been anywhere else than standing in front of Jen.

Sean found his voice finally, and in his thick Irish drawl said, "For three years, you told me about God's love. Now I've seen Him."

Heidi and Rolland often reached out to the homeless, and many of them had become their friends. In fact they had eighteen people living with them in their one-bedroom flat in London. They had partitioned off a section of the hallway with two sets of bunk beds, where Heidi, Rolland, Elisha, and Crystalyn slept, giving themselves the smallest part of their own flat.

A week later Jen knocked on the door to their flat; someone from the streets must have told her where Heidi lived. Heidi was hesitant to open the door to her, but then she noticed that Jen was holding a dozen pink roses in her hand. When Heidi opened the door, Jen began to cry, sputtering out words between heaving sobs. "Here you go...I'm so sorry I tried to kill you, but I love you too."

Heidi and Rolland and the rest of the members of their community prayed for Jen then. They also prayed for Sean, and they continued to reach out to them both.

Heidi and Rolland had not developed any real concept of a rehabilitation program. They didn't look at it like that at all, really. No one wanted to be a project; they just wanted to be family, and Jen quickly became part of the Bakers' ever-growing family. After weeks and months of love and kindness, hatred and pain began to seep out of Jen, and soon she moved off the streets and into her very own flat.

The Bakers started a church for their community, which now included some of Heidi and Rolland's fellow classmates and professors, a few lawyers, and many street sleepers like Sean. The university students thought they were just helping Heidi and Rolland at first, but they soon found themselves part of the same family as Jen and Sean.

One of the guys who partnered with Heidi and Rolland

was studying law. "People like me had no intention of getting involved," he said. Because Heidi and Rolland seemed to need help, various people like him began pitching in. They started by meeting every Saturday evening to cook food to take to the streets. He remembers Heidi removing the racks from her oven so she could fill it with as many baked potatoes as possible—hundreds of them that took hours to bake. When they were ready, the team would cut them open, fill them with baked beans, and wrap them in foil. They also took along tea and coffee; the homeless liked it because it was a hot meal.

Heidi and the team would sit down on the streets beside the homeless, befriending them and learning their stories week after week. Sometimes they invited them to the church gatherings held in Heidi and Rolland's apartment. A friend of the Bakers' remembers visiting them in their flat in London. There were so many needy people living there, Rolland and Heidi had only a tiny section of hallway left for their own family of four. Heidi's friend exclaimed, "You can't live like this!" Heidi assured her they were fine and had plenty of room.

While Heidi enjoyed her time in the lectures of some of the foremost theologians in the world, she feels like her real education came from the poor of London because the ones who are desperate are the ones who are actually hungry for God.

Heidi learned especially from Sean. Watching his transformation was such a privilege. "I just loved that man; I had this love for him that I can't explain," Heidi remembers. At first, when Sean would attend their church services, he cussed and talked through the entire meeting. There were other guys like Sean as well, men who wanted to shock and disrupt the meetings. One was a man who tried to intimidate Heidi with the pet rat he would let drink off of his tongue. Heidi, trying to break down his wall, walked over and complimented the man on his pet rat.

"That's a cute rat," she told the man, as she stroked the rat's back. It was her way of saying to the man, "Let's be friends."

When the group grew too large, they found another place to meet in the city. They moved frequently because they were kicked out of one place or another due to their ragtag bunch. First, in the London Healing Mission, which was mostly a white, middle-class group, Sean slammed the door so hard the stained glass window shattered. The repairs cost $250, which Heidi and Rolland paid. Next, the group was kicked out of King's College Refectory because some of the men hid during the service and, after everyone left, broke into the bar, drinking it dry. Sean was one of them.

When Sean saw that despite his misbehavior—despite the broken door and the money the Bakers had to pay and the incident with the alcohol—he was still loved and still part of the family, he slowly began to change. And then just like Jen, he moved into his own flat.

Just like in any family there were personalities and eccentricities in their eclectic group of about 120 people. Even Heidi was teased when she played her electric harp during the worship time. Everyone said the harp sounded awful, but as one man assured, it was not because of Heidi's inability but because of the harp itself. When someone accidentally dropped it, the harp broke. "The team was thrilled to bits," one of the former group attendees said, laughing good-naturedly. Heidi was devastated and prayed for God to fix her harp. When someone bought her another one, all they could do was laugh.

Life on the streets was easy compared to life in the university, however, where Heidi was attending classes taught by world-famous theologians who thought they knew everything. Heidi felt ill-prepared. It seemed her ability was in question, and no other woman had ever received a doctorate in the program in which she was enrolled. Heidi was scared. Had God brought her here to fail?

She walked for hours alone in the green parks of London, thinking about what she could possibly write for her dissertation that hadn't already been covered in two thousand years of church history. One day, while praying in the park, she had a vision that reassured her. She saw her famous male theologian professors shaking their heads and stroking their beards. They were puzzled and slightly annoyed. "How did that foolish woman get such wisdom?" they asked one another. She knew then that she would pass, and all she could do was laugh.

During her third year Heidi's advisor recommended she work with a female professor who would oversee her dissertation. However, at their first meeting, this particular professor ridiculed her. This didn't help Heidi's confidence in her abilities, the self-consciousness still lingering from her childhood days of dyslexia. She worried about not passing after the four years she spent in the PhD program. It would be disgraceful.

The professor told her she had "no right to be doing a PhD at King's College if [she] was not going to write about women's issues." The female academic could barely contain her anger and disdain.

But Heidi wanted to write about glossolalia, commonly known as speaking in tongues. She knew it was mostly a Pentecostal or Charismatic experience, and she knew that what she had experienced when she was sixteen years old was as real as God gets. She wanted to understand it theologically. In simple terms she wanted to write about tongues as a form of kenosis, which meant an emptying out. Her theory was that glossolalia emptied the person of himself so that an infilling of the Holy Spirit could occur. It was the divine exchange: mortality for immortality.

Trying not to cry as the woman screamed at her, Heidi

tried to explain: "In my church tradition, women don't face the same discrimination you're talking about." She thought of Aimee Semple McPherson, who led a large group of people in the 1920s and 1930s and founded the Foursquare Church. Then there was Kathryn Kuhlman, the great healing evangelist. Heidi also looked to Mother Teresa as an example. No one limited them because of their sex. Heidi didn't say any of this to her professor though.

She said, "I'm not interested in writing about women. I'm free. I've given up my rights."

Heidi defended her dissertation and was the first woman to receive her PhD from King's College London. She had worked on it from early morning to late evening every day for more than a year. She was one of two students to receive the PhD from the program that year.

Part III

Journey to Mozambique

Chapter 10

MAPUTO

COMPLETING HER PHD was demanding work for Heidi, both intellectually and emotionally, and by the end of the process she was exhausted. Heidi often joked that she was so tired that all she wanted to do was get a job at Kmart, where she wouldn't even have to brush her hair. But she had a sense God had something else for her when Rolland read to her a *TIME* magazine article about rebels blowing up Red Cross trucks in Mozambique, Africa, and she had a sudden desire to go.

While certainly different from academia, moving to Mozambique did not offer the rest that Heidi needed. In fact the country was in a state of turmoil, just beginning to recover from centuries of hardships.

In the late fourteenth century the Portuguese first traveled to Mozambique. It was a rich land: green, wild, and shining. From then on many Europeans used Mozambique's ports as a halfway point to India and the East, and trade was booming. Some Portuguese settled down and married Mozambican women and became *prazo*-holders, owning vast stretches of farmland.[1]

In the late 1800s things began to change. The Portuguese no longer adopted a Mozambican way of life but began making the Mozambicans adopt their ways: their architecture, style of business, and homeland.

This was during what is known as the Scramble for Africa in the late 1800s and early 1900s. King Leopold of Belgium invited France, England, Portugal, and a few other countries to a series of meetings at which they discussed who would get what African territory; they literally carved up the massive continent of Africa for themselves. All the resources—gold, diamonds, minerals, rubber, etc.—would go to Europe, and they would build their empires with these resources and on the backs of the Africans. It was quite possibly the biggest theft in the history of the world. Portugal claimed Mozambique as its own.[2]

The Europeans had no respect for African customs or clans as they carved up the territory. In many newly contrived "countries," opposing people groups were often unintentionally grouped together, causing severe tribal conflicts and even civil wars in the years to come. Some social scientists say Belgium (which colonized Rwanda from 1918 to 1962) exacerbated and perhaps even created the ethnic conflict that was one of the causes of the 1994 Rwandan genocide, during which almost a million people died in just a few months.[3]

Prior to colonization, explorers and missionaries had been sent to map out the territories and to see the land and its inhabitants. Their stated goal was to educate and bring religion to the people who, they thought, lived like beasts in the forest.

Many who made the journey from Europe to Africa to explore the land never came back; they were lost in the bush, eaten by crocodiles or wild animals, or overcome by some deadly disease. Missionaries who went to Africa in the 1800s never expected to see their families again. Once they set foot in Africa, their life expectancy was three years.

Rolland was still working on his dissertation when Heidi finished her degree, so they couldn't all move immediately, but he did want to visit the country before Heidi moved there.

While Heidi stayed with their kids in the UK, Rolland traveled to Mozambique to see what the conditions were like. The country had been closed to visitors for years because of a civil war, but the war had finally ended in 1992 when the government party in power, signed a peace accord with the opposing party.

Though the war was over, conditions were still rough. Many of the former soldiers had become bandits, and the country's HIV-infection rate was the tenth highest in the world. Children flooded the streets. Schools, hospitals, roads, and bridges had been destroyed, and over a million land mines had been planted.

At the time Rolland visited, almost two million refugees who had sought asylum in neighboring countries were busy returning to Mozambique. This event was part of the largest repatriation in sub-Saharan Africa, and an additional four million people, who had been internally displaced from the civil war, were returning to their homes.[4]

Rolland says he was the least likely person to be a missionary, because he was a scientist who loved research. He had grown up on the mission field (in his family there had been three generations of missionaries before him), and he didn't think it was for him. He was passionate about protons and electrons, and on his high school career and personality tests he scored the lowest on service jobs. He was not a natural people person. While he admired missionaries like his grandfather, Rolland thought he would never make a great missionary, so he decided at a young age to pursue science.

On Rolland's first visit to Mozambique his plan was to fly into South Africa and then drive across the border to Mozambique. The border closed at 5:00 p.m., and he was running late. The sun was already setting, casting long shadows on the green landscape. Minutes before arriving at the border, the truck he was driving began to fail. The engine whined and the truck slowed. He punched the gas pedal. The truck would slowed even more. He was not going to make it in time. Just before the border, the engine began whining again, apparently dying this time. It was as if there were water in the gas tank. He inched into the border station.

When he arrived, the station was in an uproar. People were shouting. Guards ran toward his truck, screaming, "The car ahead of you was just shot up by bandits. We're picking up the wounded now." If his truck's engine had run normally, he too would have been attacked as soon as he crossed the border.

There was still a line of people crossing the border by foot, and the border would be open for a few more minutes, but it was an easy decision. He would wait until the next morning when he could cross safely with a convoy of cars. Though it was three years after the war had officially ended, Mozambique was not yet a safe country.

When he turned the truck around to leave the border station, the engine ran perfectly. He knew better than to think it mere coincidence.

The next day, when he crossed the border and traveled to Maputo in a convoy, Rolland noticed the road was littered with bomb craters, and he looked warily at the bandits lining the road waiting to hijack foreigners' cars. The retired soldiers were now the police force, who received no salary and therefore had no food to feed their families, but they did have a lot of bullets—and there were enough foreigners driving by.

As Rolland drove into Mozambique, he was aware that he and Heidi were about to do what his grandfather had done in Asia: they were about to find isolated people way out in the dark, the ones nobody else cared about, the ones who never see anything good happen to them. It would be something to show the rest of the world what God could do for this isolated people.

After Rolland visited the country, he and Heidi agreed that she would move to Mozambique while Rolland stayed and finished his dissertation and cared for their children. Heidi had always been attracted to the most broken places and people. In fact, she couldn't resist them, and it seemed no place was more desperate than Mozambique. Despite the danger, she wanted to go now; she certainly didn't want to hang around the UK for six more months, possibly even a year, while Rolland wrote. Though she had many virtues, patience wasn't one them.

When Heidi left for Mozambique, she had only enough money for her airfare to South Africa and a used vehicle she would use to drive the six or seven hours to Maputo, Mozambique. She had no idea what she would do when she arrived in Mozambique. She didn't have a place to stay, and she didn't know anyone in the country. It had been twenty years since Jesus had spoken to her about one day going to Africa, and now she would be living in one of the most desperate places on the continent, alone, until Rolland came.

When she first arrived in Maputo, she stayed at a local Bible college a friend told her about. She spent the days discovering the city. Everywhere she went, Heidi noticed the multitudes of street kids. At first, she didn't know how to approach them. She remembers thinking, "I don't do children. I can sit in a university, and I can teach, but I don't know what to do with kids." Soon she was seeking them out, trying to talk to them. She didn't know what else to do but introduce herself as best she could and sit with them. Of course, she couldn't speak Shangaana, so as she sat with them on the war-torn streets, she made it a goal to learn their language.

She felt tremendous compassion for their desperate situation but wasn't sure what she could actually do to help them.

On the streets Heidi met kids like Julia, an adolescent girl who was disabled. Heidi remembers Julia moving her small body close, as if she were afraid and looking for protection. Julia used to live with her grandmother and brothers in the village, but when Julia was badly injured in a cooking fire that burned their house down, her grandmother told Julia's brothers that she was useless and to kill her. So Julia's brothers stoned her and left her lying in the tall brown weeds, thinking she was dead. Julia spent six months in the hospital recovering. No one came to visit. When the hospital finally released her, she lived on the streets. The only way she knew to survive was to offer her body to men, who paid her with a piece of bread or a Coca-Cola.

Not long after she arrived, Heidi was sitting on a street corner when an older woman wearing a long skirt and sneakers approached her. "I knew she was a missionary because of her flowered skirt, tennis shoes, and long gray hair pulled up into a bun," Heidi said.

"Can you help me?" the woman asked her.

"Of course, I can. I have nothing else to do," Heidi replied.

"Good," the woman said, tossing her house keys to her. "Watch my house and eat the food or the rats will get it. I have to go to the north." And with that, she rushed away.

Heidi, with the keys in her hand, wondered where the woman lived. She hadn't given her an address before rushing away. When she found someone who knew the address of the odd-looking white woman, Heidi fell into the house relieved, thinking, *No one will shoot at me tonight.*

Six weeks later the missionary returned, and Heidi still didn't have a long-term plan. She had gotten to know the kids; they were teaching her their language as she hung out on the street corners with them. They always showed her the places where they slept at night, usually in an alleyway or under a shop's awning. A few of them slept at the government-run children's center. An acquaintance had recently told her the government wanted to get rid of the children's center because they didn't have sufficient funds to run it.

The facility was the largest center for orphaned and abandoned children in Maputo, and Heidi's acquaintance asked her if she and Rolland wanted the children's center.

Rolland's grandparents had run a children's center in China, so it was appealing to both Heidi and Rolland for that reason. After all, they had come to help, and the orphaned and abandoned kids were some of the neediest. How could they say no?

They didn't know where they would get the money to run it, but they would figure that out later.

The first step was visiting the children's center. When Heidi saw it, she was shocked and tempted to wonder if there could possibly be enough hope and love for this place. She had never seen conditions like these: the children had bloated bellies and bumps all over their skin from scabies, caused by an infestation of tiny mites. The children lived in conditions hardly fit for animals—no wonder they did not know how to smile.

Heidi started visiting every day, spending most of her time with the children. She always took them food. As the weeks and then months passed, she made as many small repairs as she could. She brought the kids whatever she could think of—and afford—that would improve their quality of life.

The kids were delighted with the blonde woman who gave them candy; even more, they were relieved to have someone who played and laughed with them instead of hurt them. The previous directors of the center awakened them each day at 4:00 a.m. so they could begin gathering wood for cooking or find water for bathing and drinking. The children experienced cruelty, though they were not quite sure why they were being beaten several times a day.

But the children didn't have to do anything to please the blonde American woman. She was always smiling at them, and she even bought them their first toothbrushes, plates, and cups.

In light of this the government wanted to hand the center over to Heidi. When Rolland arrived in the country, he and Heidi assumed total responsibility for the center and began completely remodeling the place, installing wiring, cleaning septic tanks, and painting.

Even then Heidi still went to the streets of Maputo each week to visit the street kids she had befriended, and every time she brought more of them home with her to the newly remodeled children's center. She loved being able to give children like Julia a real home.

Someone from one of the churches in Maputo said to her: "If you insist on being a missionary here and working with children, at least work with ones who have some hope. These kids are street urchins and bandits, and they'll never be any different."

"I think they're the most beautiful treasures on the face of the planet," she replied.

One of those treasures was a small boy named Juma. When Heidi found him living on the street in downtown Maputo, he was crying pitifully. It was more of a constant whine, as if he had no tears left. Juma looked sick and was probably dehydrated. Heidi took him to the doctor, who said he would probably die from the double pneumonia and other diseases he had.

Not only was he very sick, but Juma was also very angry, lashing out and hitting everyone who came near him. He didn't know how old he was or what his parents had named him; Juma was what his friends called him. It was hard to tell what kinds of abuse he had suffered as a young boy living on the street in a war-torn country. Most street kids just were trying to survive.

Heidi remembers the day she brought Juma home to her house. Instead of taking him into the dorm-like housing, she brought him into her own home. She did this for each new child so they could bathe and eat a warm meal; she wanted them to feel they had a home with her.

At first Juma couldn't communicate. Heidi pulled his small, thin body into her arms, holding his hands so he couldn't hit her, and she rocked him while he cried silent tears. Heidi tried not to think about how he could have been beaten and raped or what might have happened to his parents. But his constant mourning told her all she needed to know, so Heidi held him in her arms day after day; week after week, she rocked him whenever she could.

When Juma was out of her sight, he tried to steal anything he could get his hands on. "Juma was a little rascal," Heidi said. "He would steal everything."

One day, though, Juma stopped fighting with the other children, and it was the last time he stole anything. It was the day he finally relaxed into Heidi's soft arms. It was a gradual change in personality, but Juma became a happy child, one who played with the others and laughed all the time.

Someone from the outside might not understand the cause of Juma's healing, but love is something as tangible as clinical therapy, and Heidi had discovered its real and transformative power through the years. Where God's supernatural love was, nothing else could remain. Love did more than just drive away fear; it drove away everything else until all that was left was the feeling of being safe, delighted in, and free.

Miguel, an Iris pastor who worked with Heidi and Rolland, had watched Juma's transformation closely, and when he saw what individual attention and care had done for him, Pastor Miguel decided to adopt Juma as his own child. He took him home to live with his family, and he became Juma's new papa.

Juma continued to attend Iris's new school, a school that would soon be recognized as the best in the nation with the highest exam scores. And after Pastor Miguel adopted him, Juma became the top student in the school! "He got the top scores because the spirit of adoption hit him," Heidi told me.

The Iris school was filled with kids who were once on the street—from hospitals, institutions, and abused backgrounds— but who were now mostly like Juma. They lit up a room.

Heidi told me about Juma in a way that made me think he was one of her favorite kids, that this was one of her favorite transformational stories. Truth is, they all seemed to be her favorite.

Juma was one of a hundred favorites. The children in the center were learning that they were safe and that their basic needs would be met; they were learning to receive love; they were learning practical skills as they attended school for the first time in their lives.

Heidi told their stories as if they were part of a larger story. "We are all adopted into a family," she preached. Heidi had seen her little street kids start to become leaders, and she loved to brag about them. "Twelve thousand applicants for two spaces left in the university; guess who got in? Two of our kids. I love it!" she said, laughing exuberantly at the fact that her kids were welcomed into Maputo's only university.

Caring for these beautiful children was the most fulfilling thing Heidi had done so far. She loved seeing lives transformed; it gave her such incredible joy, and the kids had a world of potential and were coming to life before her eyes. Rolland also seemed to be enjoying the adventure of living in

Mozambique and the huge family they were building together. Now that they had overcome the initial obstacles of getting the children's center remodeled and running smoothly, everyone was blossoming, including themselves.

But they had no idea of the challenges just ahead.

Chapter 11

MULTIPLICATION

NITIALLY THE GOVERNMENT hadn't wanted these children because they didn't have the resources to properly care for them. But when they saw the remodeled children's center and the repairs the Bakers had made, they realized they could benefit from them. The country was barely recovering from decades of chaos, and there was no order. Everything was based on self-interest. If the government officials thought they could benefit from something, they would do what they could to get that benefit.

One day when Heidi walked into the warehouse where they stored the food, she found it completely empty—the food was gone. Someone had stolen it; all that was left was ketchup and herbal tea. "What am I going to do with this ketchup?" she wondered as she stood there looking around at the huge, empty warehouse.

The former directors of the children's center apparently still had a key to the building and must have come in during the night, and the ketchup and tea were the only things they didn't want.

Heidi was so desperate to feed the children that for a second she actually thought they might be able to eat the ketchup: Could they put the ketchup on sticks and the children lick it off? There was nothing else. She knew they would not drink the herbal tea; she hadn't met a Mozambican who didn't hate tea without sugar.

Heidi didn't know what to do, so she began to pray. She

thought about the privilege it was to be surrounded by the children and to see their transformations one by one. These were the same children others had called worthless, but God was showing her how valuable they were to Him. She wasn't going to give up on them.

When the sun began to sink lower into the horizon, the rays casting orange shadows over the desolate land, Heidi was beginning to worry. They were all hungry, and they had nothing to eat and no money for food. She knew it wouldn't be long before the night came and the machine gun fire started. People wanted to scare them away, so each evening when it grew dark, they would shoot into the air outside their windows.

Heidi had long ago grown weary of the machine gun fire, but tonight it seemed she had even less patience for it.

As Heidi was pondering the situation, a truck with four passengers pulled into their driveway. "Are you Mama Aida?" the Mozambican driver asked.

"Yes," she said, wondering who the men were and what they wanted.

"We have food for you. Where do you want it?"

Heidi watched in amazement as the four men loaded food, piles and piles of it, into the warehouse. The truck was full of cornmeal and rice and beans and sugar. The kids would have sugar for their tea tonight! The truck came only that once, and Heidi had no idea who had sent it or where it had come from.

The theft of the food wouldn't be their last run-in with the government. After winning a ten-year struggle for independence from Portugal in 1975, the ruling party of Mozambique turned to the Socialist bloc of countries for international aid and installed a one-party government in Mozambique, which created a long civil war. At the signing of the peace accord in the early nineties, the United Nations sent in peacekeeping forces to oversee a transition to democracy.

With the first successful free elections in 1994, the last members of the UN peacekeeping force were just leaving as Rolland and Heidi arrived in Mozambique, but the streets were still a dangerous place to be. Threads of atheism and anti-Christian sentiment ran strong. Not only did the government frown upon anything Christian, but they also realized they would be losing money—all the aid money that came in from the Red Cross and various other organizations for the children's center—now that they had given the Bakers the children's center.

Not only did the government order the Bakers to leave the children's center, but they also placed a bounty on Heidi. The bounty reward was the equivalent of twenty US dollars.

"I was mad," Heidi told me. "Certainly I'm worth more than twenty dollars," she joked.

One of Heidi's friends, Elias, who had fought in the civil war and then worked in the children's center, came to her. "Don't worry, Mama. I have a plan." As he promised to protect her, she smiled at him.

"Don't you worry, Mama. I'm a solider," he said. "I have an AK-47 and a grenade under my bed. I will go and kill them." He thought she was going to be happy about that. "I love you, Mama. I'm going to kill them," he repeated.

"Leave me for a moment," she said, looking at his beaming face. Fight or turn the other cheek? War or pacifism? It was not an intellectual decision or a theological discussion, but possibly her life.

She came back to Elias to gently tell him no. She did not need his help. Then she spoke to the children during dinner in the kitchen, and she told them the same thing: "We are here to love, and I want to live in love. We'll be blessed for being peacemakers, and we will be called sons and daughters of God. I want you to love those who want to hurt us. I want you to love them without limit, without bottom."

She preached with everything she had, vowing to never change her message. Love was all she had; it was that simple.

But this meant they would have to leave the center. They had no money and nowhere to go but the small office Rolland had rented in the city, so at 2:00 a.m., under the cover of darkness, Heidi gathered the youngest children, the ones who were too small to walk, along with her biological children. "We've got to go now, children," she whispered to them as she put them into the back of the one truck they owned while Rolland pushed it out of the driveway so no one would hear them leaving. It was especially dangerous at night because bandits were everywhere, waiting to wreak havoc. People who owned cars were considered wealthy, so Rolland knew he had to be hyper vigilant as he drove them into their office in the city.

The children's center that had become their home would be confiscated the next morning, and the children they hadn't been able to take with them—they didn't know what would happen to them. All Heidi could do was pray. In deep and painful contemplation she mouthed silent words of prayer for her children.

The next day soldiers forced their way into the center where the rest of the kids were gathered in the kitchen for breakfast. Grown men in military fatigues faced a ragtag group of children. The children, not knowing what else to do, began to dance and sing: "*Kanimambo, xikwembo. Alelua, Alelua xikwembo.* (God is great; we thank You, God. You're so great. You're wonderful. Hallelujah.)"

"You children," one of the men spat, "If you want food, you will close your mouths."

They kept singing.

"If you want a place to live, you will close your mouths, and you will not worship God. He does not exist. If you worship Him, you will starve to death. We are willing to feed you. We are willing to take over this center; we will give you food. God does not exist. If you read the Bible, if you pray, even by yourself under a tree, you will starve to death."

The children ignored the men and continued singing, "*Kanimambo...*" They remembered what Mama Aida had said to them the night before, and they knew they were loved.

The men slapped some of the boys in the face, and when the kids ran out into the red dirt, still singing, the military men, now furious, chased them, throwing rocks at the back of their heads.

The children did not fight back.

"Foolish...idiots," the soldiers called after the children as they left through the wide-open front gate.

The kids walked over seventeen miles on dirt roads, barefoot, until they got to the city and finally reached Rolland and Heidi's office. Not one of them stayed at the children's center. One boy wondered how his grandmother would find him when she came to visit him at the center; he was tempted to stay just for her, but even he knew he had to go away from the men in uniforms who tried to hurt them. One by one, two by two, and in groups as large as ten, they walked to the place Heidi and Rolland were staying. Many had bleeding feet from the arduous walk.

Not having any other option, the Bakers took them into the office and laid out straw mats in the small courtyard. Almost two hundred of them squeezed into the office and courtyard until there was not a place to step but over bodies. There was only one bathroom.

Heidi and Rolland were beyond themselves. In the natural world they had absolutely no way to care for the two hundred children who were now theirs. When the kids arrived at their office in the city on foot, they knew they had to do something, but they were completely overwhelmed.

Heidi was angry. While theologically she knew she was loved, this did not feel like love. This did not feel like God was taking care of her or her children. She would certainly take care of her kids better if she could.

Heidi had always felt that her relationship with God was about "love, a deep love that captured her heart," but she hadn't eaten or slept for days, and she felt like her heart was breaking. She had no idea where God was. They were out of options.

"Then God came and did the first incredible miracle I had ever seen," Heidi told me.

The missionary woman who had left Heidi her house for six weeks at the beginning of Heidi's time in Mozambique visited them at their office. "Hi, honey, I brought you some food for your family," she said, speaking Portuguese with a Southern accent.

She gasped when she saw the Mozambican children all over the courtyard. She hadn't known the children had followed Heidi and Rolland. Though the Bakers had found temporary housing for many of the children, there still were so many of them! The missionary had brought rice and chili, but it was only enough to feed Heidi's family of four—at the most eight if one dished out tiny portions.

"Thank you, sweetheart, but I have a big family," Heidi said simply, looking the woman in the eye and then at the hundreds of kids that surrounded them.

"No," the missionary replied. "This is for you, for *your* family."

"Thank you." There was nothing else to do but share the food, even if it meant it would soon run out.

The missionary was furious, feeling obligated to go and make more food. "Let me go make more then," she said resentfully.

"No, no, you're here already," Heidi said with resignation. She didn't want to impose.

"Why are you doing this?" the missionary demanded.

"We have a big family. Just bless the food. I'm hungry. I'm tired; the kids walked all day. Just pray," Heidi said, desperate. She had studied systematic theology for ten years, she knew the stories she had been reading since she was sixteen, and she believed nothing was impossible. But still, she had never seen a miracle of this magnitude with her own eyes.

"God bless it," the missionary said doubtfully, looking again at her meager meal, perhaps now wishing she had just stayed at home.

There was a little pot of rice and a little pot of chili.

Somehow each child ate—every one of the fifty or so who remained with Heidi and Rolland. Heidi even began to enjoy scooping out generous amounts for each one. Almost recklessly she handed out the food. She did not give small portions because they were hungry, reasoning that there had been twelve basketfuls of leftovers in the Bible story.

She was discovering that all she had to do was believe the way a child would, the way her children did.

The boy who had been thinking of staying at the children's center to wait for his grandmother remembers the multiplication of the food. "I didn't know what happened. I just thought it was magic or something."

Soon, a friend of the Bakers found new property for them to rent, allowing them to move the kids out of the small office. It was in a large open area in the countryside, but they had a lot of work to do. The land needed to be cleared of brush, there were many snakes that needed to be removed, and there was a lot of construction to do because there were no buildings at all on the property, which meant they would need to believe God for even bigger miracles.

Chapter 12

THE BOCARIA

O NE OF HEIDI's friends, Bre, was coming to visit them in Mozambique around the same time they were constructing their new center. Bre had known Heidi a long time; they met when they were young mothers and had both been dancers.

Through the years Bre kept in touch with Heidi and read her newsletters with deep curiosity. When Heidi wrote that she and Rolland were going to Africa, Bre read the letter and reread it. She felt a twinge of desire to go herself. As a teenager Bre had a vision of herself wearing a bandana and surrounded by African children. At the time she thought, *Maybe I'll work with the poor one day.* Bre hadn't thought of that vision for years until she heard from Heidi: "We're called to the poorest country, and we're going."

Bre wondered if she should visit, but when she read Heidi's stories of their lives being threatened and being kicked out of their children's center with nowhere to go, two hundred children following them on foot for miles, she thought maybe it wasn't a good time. It could be dangerous.

Nevertheless Bre decided to visit for several weeks shortly after Heidi and Rolland had moved into their new center in Maputo. Bre remembers almost every detail of her first experience of Mozambique because it changed everything—not only the way she performed but also her perception of life.

At that time the center consisted of just one house and a dorm for the babies. Because the war had ended only a few years before, there were no paved roads. Instead, there were only dirt lanes marked by potholes that would swallow a tire.

The airport was craziness, with everyone coming at Bre, wanting to grab her bags. The officers at customs all wanted a bribe. In fact, everyone wanted a bribe. Heidi arrived at the airport and told the men harassing Bre to go away.

"Thank God she spoke their language," Bre told me. "We get to her truck and Heidi shows us the bullet hole a couple of inches from the gas tank, and she's explaining what we do in case we get stopped by the Mozambican police because they all want bribes. I thought, *Lord please protect me; I have little children at home. Do I really know what I'm getting myself into?*

When they arrived at the center, the kids ran up and hugged Bre, and then stepped away to examine her with big, wide grins while they chattered away in their native language. None of them knew English. Once she was surrounded by children, suddenly she didn't care about the danger or the heat or any of the discomforts. It was as if long ago she had somehow seen herself in the future, surrounded by these children. She put on her bandana to keep the sweat from dripping into her eyes.

Heidi wanted her to teach the kids to dance, but Bre found it difficult because she didn't know the language. The first thing she needed to do was learn to count to eight in Portuguese. When she had learned her numbers, she taught them a very simple dance. It was all she could teach them. When Heidi went to the streets to hand out food and spend time with people who lived there, she wanted the kids to perform the dance for them.

The dance certainly drew attention and humbled Bre, the trained dancer. She watched as the crowds came: the prostitutes and drug addicts, the street kids, and anyone else who was around. They gathered in close so they could see. The smells were unlike anything she had smelled before: the smell of food gone sour mixed with hints of urine and sweat.

Bre didn't know if the people even understood what was going on, but she reminded herself that dance was universal. When she didn't have the words to express herself, she would do a movement and the kids would smile and do the same movement, and then she felt they were speaking the same language after all.

After the street ministry they followed Heidi to the *bocaria*, a trash dump where Heidi and Rolland led a small church.

"Here is this place that is filthy dirty, with biting flies everywhere. The stench is horrid, and Heidi is just in her sandals walking right through," Bre said. "I'm thinking this is gross, disgusting. I have these huge boots on because I'm scared to death of everything. Heidi is just trudging through, inviting people to come to the church they have on the little mud slab in the middle of the trash dump."

Bre learned from Heidi how to not be afraid to walk through people's trash to get to them, literally and metaphorically.

There was a huge dead rat on its back in the piles of garbage. *Even the rats are dying*, Bre thought. She watched, shuddering in horror, as the trash truck ran over the dead rat and people flocked to pick through the new trash.

She noticed a little girl who was about six or seven years old. The small girl, who had bumps on her arms and legs from scabies, picked up a doll from the trash and draped it over her shoulder as if it were a baby. It had two legs and only one arm attached to its body, but the girl held onto it like it was the treasure of her life.

"It just broke me," Bre said. "I watched Heidi reaching out to these people and loving on these ladies and inviting them to church, and they all came down to the church as if it were a special event and they were the guests of honor."

As Bre, Heidi, and the ladies all carefully made their way down onto the cement slab, Bre watched silently, trying to absorb this experience. She saw a large lizard crawl up the side of the slab. More than anything else, the lizard made her feel way outside of her comfort zone.

There Heidi was in the middle of it all. Heidi turned to Bre, "Do you think you could, just whatever happens, do a little dance for them?"

"I'm like, 'Sure, here I am in my hiking boots.'"

Heidi played some beautiful music from a small CD player. Bre laughed about doing ballet in her boots, but the people just smiled at her.

Bre thought, *This is just such a surrender. This is it.* Her concept of performance and what a stage was supposed to be like was shattered. It was as if someone were saying to her: "Here and now, this is it; this is your best audience ever. If you can dance here in the trash dump, you can dance before anyone."

She smiled back at their beaming faces, surrendered, and performed ballet in her hiking boots. "I have a picture of them, the people who live in the trash dump, worshipping, their arms up, faces lit, singing," Bre told me. "It is the biggest irony of life—how one can live in a trash dump and have the most joy."

Afterward they fed everyone. Bre helped pass out the food and she loved watching the kids come to eat. She could see that they were hungry by the way they shoved fistfuls of food into their tiny mouths.

After they ate, everyone was trying to do ballet, even a man who had once tried to kill Heidi with a broken glass bottle. Someone turned the music on again, and they stood in the middle of the trash dump together, moving and dancing. That's when Bre felt like she was at a wedding reception, where people dance in celebration. In the poorest place in the world she was experiencing a glimpse of heaven.

One of the first times I saw Heidi in action in Mozambique was at the same city dump in Maputo that Bre had visited years earlier. Heidi was there because a film crew from Hollywood who was filming a documentary about land mines left over from the civil war had requested her presence. After they had seen a documentary based on her life and work in Mozambique, titled *Mama Heidi,* they thought she would be helpful for her contacts and ability to speak the languages of the people the crew needed to interview.

They wanted to get some shots in the garbage dump, and Heidi was more than familiar with the place. Heidi introduced everyone to Vidal, the man who tried to kill her with a broken Coke bottle. He had been drunk and stuck the jagged glass to her throat. "Get out of my dump, white woman," he said. "I'm going to kill you. White woman...taking my garbage."

She had been nervous, of course, as the sharp edge touched her skin. She could smell the alcohol on Vidal's breath. She spoke to him kindly and softly, convincing him she was not taking anything from him. When she told Vidal about Jesus, he asked her if Jesus could come to the dump to visit so he could meet Him. She explained who Jesus was and the sacrifice He made for him, and Vidal's life changed that day. Real love did that. Now Heidi and Vidal were friends.

As I rode with the camera crew around and then through the dump, I saw kids wading through a sea of garbage, some of it still burning from the night before, smoke stinging their eyes, swarming flies biting. We passed shacks where people sold fruit, and from the car window the black bananas looked like misshapen pieces of charcoal.

Arriving at the back of the dump, I climbed out at Iris's church, where Heidi was passing out four kilos of rice, a kilo of beans, and a long loaf of bread to each person. I observed

Heidi closely in this extreme environment. She bent down to look the children in the eyes and to smile at them. She hugged each person, squeezing the children to her, seemingly oblivious to the flies, the stench, the heat of the sun, and the sweat that dripped from her face. Her black eyeliner was melting, forming a small puddle under her bright blue eyes. It was as if her hugs meant more than any other person's hugs would, as if they were a sort of prayer for a better life for each one she touched.

The film crew was setting up for an interview with Heidi, and after Heidi answered the interviewer's questions about her work in the dump, the large camera focused on the interviewer: "Leonel has an unbelievable story," the interviewer said in a loud, overly dramatic voice. "The plastic mines floated to the top in the floods and blew him up when he was hoeing his garden."

Leonel, the young Mozambican man Heidi had known since he was a boy, sat in the corner by the fence with his bag of rice. His face had been severely burned, scarred pink like the color of his pale pink hat. He stared down into the loaf of bread he was holding as if he were bored. Leonel was one of the boys Heidi had taken into her home many times. He always ran away, but not because he didn't like his new home with Heidi; he loved it. Trouble was, because of his dramatic scars, he made a lot of money begging on the streets.

Heidi didn't seem to like the camera very much, but I got the impression that she wanted to help the kids of Mozambique badly enough to do whatever it took to interest the rest of the world. These children were living in extreme poverty; this was one of the pockets of the world where the people actually lived on less than a dollar a day, starving and sick, dying of disease and lack of clean water and all the usual clichés. Heidi was smart enough to know the West would not be swayed by cliché; perhaps seeing the poverty through her eyes would give them a more personal experience of poverty.

Heidi was no typical spokesperson for the poor; she did not plead or beg or try to look sad. She was full of quiet joy and love, and it seemed she was actually able to transfer some of that joy to the children who had been born into this life in the dump. Their sad eyes grew brighter when she hugged them to her.

Part IV

STOPPING FOR THE ONE

Chapter 13

TORONTO

EIDI HAD BEEN a missionary for years without a furlough, and she didn't believe in fences between her and those she was serving, because she believed with all her heart that fences that walled you from people were evil—no matter that she needed a break or that she never had a moment without little brown faces peering at her, calling singsong-like, "Ma-ma Ai-daaaaa." But those physically demanding early years without a break were beginning to take their toll.

Months after their first center had been confiscated and they had moved into their new one, Heidi came down with pneumonia. Combined with her chronic fatigue syndrome, she was so weak she needed to leave Mozambique. They thought she might die if she stayed because the conditions were so harsh. The streets were still treacherous, both from war damage and from soldiers who no longer had an occupation. They now terrorized anyone they could, and corruption was rampant. For all intents and purposes Mozambique was still a war zone. It certainly wasn't the best place for someone who needed to recover.

Barely able to get on the flight, Heidi left for California. She checked herself into a hospital upon arrival in the States, and when her pneumonia dragged on and on, she decided to check herself out and fly to Toronto, Canada, where there was a church and missionary rest home she had heard about from Rolland, who had been in Toronto a few months earlier.

He had come back to Mozambique changed. He seemed happier and freer after spending time at the Toronto Airport Christian Fellowship (now Catch the Fire Toronto), which had been having ongoing revival services for over a year.

When she arrived in Toronto to visit the missionary rest home and the church, she was so sick she had to be helped into the church for the worship service. She laid down on a pew in the back, so tired that it was all she could do to listen.

Heidi was annoyed.

As she lay there, all she could think about were the carpets. She couldn't believe the church had that much carpet. Mozambique was so poor that dirt permeated everything, even the floors of the people's homes. Then her thoughts went to how much people ate in the West; it made her feel sick just thinking about it.

Heidi felt miserable.

"How could God love these people? Didn't He care about the poor?" she thought, stewing while the others worshipped.

The next day, as she lay in the back of the church during another worship service, Heidi's body began to grow warm. The heat came in waves, as if she was taking steps closer and closer to a raging fire. Soon she was drenched in sweat. Her body started vibrating, as if she was shaking from the inner core of her being.

Then she saw Jesus come to her in her mind's eye. He was surrounded by children—a huge multitude of children, more than she could count. Just looking at them and the need they represented made her tired.

She was exhausted in every way, not only from her physical ailments and the strenuous work in Mozambique, but also from the rigorous degree she had completed the year before in London.

She was surprised that when Jesus came to her during

that church service He didn't say, "Just rest, honey," as everyone else was telling her. Instead, Jesus showed her even more need. "It wasn't even nice," she told me, remembering that moment when the vision was so real. The colors were amazing, and the children—there were so many of them. Jesus looked into her eyes. She looked back, and the complexity of what she saw in His eyes overwhelmed her. It was like she saw and experienced every possible emotion all at the same time. Deeper and deeper she gazed into His eyes until all she could feel were the depths of His pain. He suffered because his children were suffering.

"I died so that there would always be enough," He said.

The words pierced her, the revelation of it—enough for her, enough for the world, enough for the children of Mozambique, enough for the poverty of Mozambique.

Then He took a piece of His flesh from His bloody side and handed it to her. "Give it to the children," He told Heidi. She just looked at Him. She peered at the bloody piece of flesh in her hand and thought of her children in Mozambique. *I can't give that to them,* she thought.

"I died so there would always be enough," He said again. She knew He was speaking about everything—physically, spiritually, emotionally—for every one of them.

As she held the flesh He had ripped out of His side, it suddenly transformed into fresh bread in her hands. She handed a piece to the child who was in front of her in the vision. Then the bread multiplied. It grew bigger the way yeast causes dough to rise, and she had enough to feed every single child.

The vision continued. Jesus now had a poor man's cup in His hands. He moved it close to His side, where bright red blood and water filled the humble cup to the brim. His eyes, filled with kindness and radiating light, watched her, admiring her as if He already knew what she would decide, but He asked anyway, "Will you drink it?"

He didn't speak with actual words, but her spirit understood His question. He was the first word, and He could communicate Spirit to spirit without using words.

"It's a cup of suffering and joy. Will you drink it?" Jesus asked again.

Suffering and joy. Everyone wanted the joy, but the suffering?

Heidi had experienced suffering to an extent. She told me that she didn't know if she could have said yes if she knew what the future held.

She took the cup, and as she touched the liquid to her lips, it turned into wine, both bitter and sweet, and then she turned and gave it to the children. They all drank. There was enough for every one of them, and she knew instantly what message she was being given: there was more need than she had even imagined. Jesus was telling her there was enough for all of it.

Heidi thought back to the time He multiplied the small pots of chili and rice, and she understood that He Himself was the Bread of Life, and His desire was to fill her and the kids and every human being who was hungry. She thought of the event in Scripture when Jesus asked the woman at the well to give Him a drink. Jesus's thirst was a symbol of a spiritual reality: that we all thirst. Humanity tried to quench this thirst in various ways, but in the end it was only love that could satisfy us.

He was offering the fullness of His all-sufficient love to the children, to the ones who had been abused and neglected, left dying in the trash dump and under trees. He wanted to feed them, to nourish them so that they would grow into beautiful sons and daughters. He gave His body to be bread for them and the entire human race. Surely there was enough for the children of Mozambique.

When the vision ended and Heidi finally got up from the

floor, she was completely healed of pneumonia and walked out as if she hadn't been ill at all. The chronic fatigue was gone too; it never came back. Heidi's full strength had returned.

———————

The money and sacrifice it took to journey to Toronto had been worth it. The cost of the airfare had seemed ridiculous, outrageous even, when considering the hundreds of children Heidi and Rolland had to feed each day. The Bakers, who never wrote anyone asking for money, lived purely on faith; they just prayed and lived lives of voluntary poverty. The cost of the trip was a sacrifice, but it was worth it.

Heidi was well acquainted with sacrifice, but during her visit to Toronto she distinctly heard the Holy Spirit tell her, "Eat cheese and take a warm bath." She thought fasting was a virtue, something in which He took pleasure. When the Holy Spirit told her to eat cheese, she couldn't believe it: "I fell apart. Eat cheese and take a warm bath? I couldn't believe God loved me that much. I didn't understand that He loved me that much. I really do like cheese. I do. And I really love warm water. That's the one thing I can handle about speaking at conferences in the West. I used to accept an invitation thinking, 'I'm going to have a bath.' I realized the Father loves me, really loves me, and I was not going to be the worst missionary the planet had ever seen if I ate cheese."

Something else happened in Toronto, something that would set the course of Heidi's life for the coming years and would give her the vision for an entire African nation. When the guest preacher, Randy Clark, spoke about spiritual hunger, Heidi began to weep.

"Are you hungry?" he asked. "Do you want what God has to give you? He can give you fresh bread from heaven to satisfy." She couldn't believe what she was hearing. It was what she had seen in her vision the day before! She knew God was speaking directly to her.

"Yes," Heidi cried, running to the front. She didn't care that there hadn't been an invitation to come to the altar yet or about the thousands of people in the room who were looking at her. At the front she knelt down on her knees and closed her eyes as she had countless times before, the way she had when she was sixteen meeting Jesus for the first time.

The preacher stopped speaking for a moment. He had never seen the blonde woman who knelt in front of him, and Heidi didn't know him either. "God wants to know," he said to Heidi, "Do you want a nation?"

Heidi began to sob. "Yes!" she said, throwing herself prostrate on the carpet.

Randy told her that the deaf would hear, the lame would walk, the blind would see.

Heidi knew this wasn't just Scripture Randy was repeating, but that God would do these things in Mozambique. She couldn't wait to get back and start praying for the sick. They were everywhere; there was only one doctor for roughly every thirty thousand people.

Heidi had yet to see with her own eyes the blind see or the deaf hear. This was years before she saw the young Mozambican boy's hearing dramatically return. But she had arrived in Toronto sick, and she was leaving healed; she knew God could and would do for others what He had done for her.

As Heidi boarded the plane out of Toronto, she felt stronger and healthier than she had in years. Heidi knew she had made the right decision to visit the church in Toronto instead of staying in the hospital in California just waiting for the pneumonia to go away.

Before returning to Mozambique, Heidi accepted an invitation to speak at a large evangelical church in the United States.

After she finished preaching, the pastor was so moved that his church wanted to commit to giving the Bakers a million dollars over the course of a year for their ministry.

This was a miracle. A million dollars would meet all of their needs for an entire year!

Heidi and Rolland could finally relax; they didn't have to wonder where the money would come from for next month's needs, and they could finally pay off their credit cards. Their ministry funds were low, and they had maxed out all of their credit cards in order to feed the children.

They were overjoyed when they received that first month's support. But then the pastor saw something online that offended him: a video of Heidi at the revival in Toronto. He was furious.

He was more conservative theologically, and when he heard that the church was experiencing revival—or renewal as some called it—he balked, and when he saw the video and the charismatic manifestations, he was downright offended.

He and Heidi were coming from two completely different theological viewpoints. The main messages that came from the Toronto church were focused on God's love, the His Father heart for His children, and healing past emotional pain. Heidi didn't understand how there could be anything wrong with those themes. But she was aware that the revival was controversial because some people questioned the manifestations attendees experienced: tears, shaking, and uncontrollable laughter.

People traveled from all over the world to the Toronto church to experience God's tangible presence, the number of visitors numbering in the millions. But some critics, like the offended pastor, dismissed what was happening in Toronto entirely, saying it wasn't God at all.

He wrote Heidi and Rolland a letter, explaining the nature

of his offense. It was obvious he wasn't willing to dialogue or consider the possibility that Heidi and Rolland had greatly benefitted from their experiences at the revival, which in turn blessed thousands of others. What was worse, he said he would not support the Bakers if they ever went to the church in Toronto again.

The tone of the letter was basically saying, "Choose a million dollars or Toronto." To the Bakers it was as if he was asking them to choose between money or God Himself.

Heidi had finally found a church that wasn't merely religious and wasn't going to just give her a set of rules to live by, but one that valued freedom, one where she was free to experience the purest, most healing love she had ever known and free to receive visions from Jesus and to speak freely about them.

If she had accepted the money from the pastor's megachurch, Heidi told me she would have felt like a spiritual prostitute, as if she had been bought with money. So Heidi and Rolland turned down the million dollars and never looked back.

Chapter 14

RESTORED SIGHT

O N HER WAY home to Mozambique, Heidi couldn't stop thinking about the vision of Jesus and His words that there was always enough. The thing that especially excited her was the new expectation that the sick would be healed. She determined to begin seeking out the blind, fully expecting to see miracles.

One day not long after she returned from Toronto, she spotted a blind man sitting on the sidewalk. When she abruptly stopped her truck in the middle of traffic, horns blared all around, but she ignored them and went to the blind beggar and introduced herself. After talking to him for a little while, Heidi asked him if she could pray for his eyes. She told him that Jesus could heal him. She prayed and kept praying, sure that God would heal this precious man.

But though she prayed for as long as she could, the blind man was not healed, and he still could not see.

Heidi's heart hurt. She wept as she held him in her arms.

For the next year Heidi continued to seek out those who were deaf and blind the way she sought out the street kids and those living in the dump—the ones who were neediest. But even though she had faith, and even though she was intentional, she saw no miracles; nothing changed.

Then one day when she was talking to God about this, she heard the small whisper: "You have not failed. You've done what I've asked you to do. Your only job is to love." In this moment Heidi realized that God just wanted her to simply show love to the person in front of her; she wasn't the one who had the power to heal; it was Jesus in her. And sometimes His ways were beyond understanding, but she would continue to trust in His goodness even when she didn't see the healings she asked for.

To this day she reminds herself of this anytime she prays for someone who doesn't receive healing. Her only job is to love. And if she loves well, she has not failed.

A year or so after Heidi returned from Toronto, she went on an outreach to a bush village in the middle of Mozambique. They had arrived in a small Cessna plane, landing in the middle of a small field with mud huts all around. Almost immediately a few of the women asked her to follow them to one particular hut; they walked for what seemed like miles until the sun was almost setting.

It was dark inside the little hut, but it didn't matter to the blind and ill woman inside. Heidi looked at the sick woman standing in front of her and spoke softly to her in the woman's own African dialect: "The Jesus who loves you wants to heal you." As Heidi prayed for her, she fell slowly backward, as if she no longer had the strength to stand, and she lay there on the solid dirt floor. Heidi continued asking God to fill and to heal this dear woman who had no option other than Jesus.

When the tiny Mozambican woman gasped, Heidi knew something was happening. The blind woman seemed to be looking at—and seeing—Heidi, the petite blonde woman who was now kneeling beside her, clasping her hand, still praying. Heidi watched the woman's eyes turn from white to gray to dark brown.

The blind woman was no longer blind. She could see, and she was healed.

Heidi was almost as surprised as the woman, whose name was Aida. Heidi thought nothing of the coincidence that they shared the same name. She was just thrilled that the woman was whole now. It had been a long journey of faith and perseverance for Heidi.

A few days later, back at home in Maputo, Heidi went to the gas station to fill her car with fuel and she met a blind man with a large tumor on his head. After just witnessing the blind woman receive her sight a few days before, Heidi thought for sure this man would be healed when she prayed for him.

Heidi prayed, but when he was not healed, she was confused.

Then she remembered Jesus's words to her about loving the person in front of her. What did love look like in this man's situation?

Heidi suddenly thought of her friend who was a surgeon on the East Coast. She phoned him, and before they finished talking, he was making plans to fly all the way to Africa to remove the man's tumor.

"He's still in church," Heidi told me triumphantly, referring to the man who had regained his sight as a result of the tumor being removed.

Heidi couldn't have been more delighted to see the body of Christ function as it was meant to. She was realizing that perhaps healing looked different in different scenarios. Maybe sometimes God chose to heal supernaturally and sometimes through doctors or medicine. Was it any less a miracle that medical doctors had been able to develop cures for diseases that we could purchase at the pharmacy?

Months later Heidi held a conference in the bush in the central part of the country around the port city of Beira. Before she preached, Heidi called for the deaf and the blind, anyone who was sick and needed healing. Many came forward because in this area there was no doctor other than the witch doctor. There were so many sick people that Heidi wondered how she would have time to actually pray for them all.

A small boy pushed and pulled his blind mother through the crowd. Heidi remembers saying: "In the name of Jesus," and again, she watched a woman's eyes change color from white to brown and then come into focus.

"Eu posso ver (I can see)," the woman said.

The crowd went wild. They shouted; they sang; they danced in celebration.

"What's your name?" Heidi asked the woman.

"Aida," she said. Heidi asked again what her name was, thinking the woman was saying Heidi's name.

"No, it's not Aida. It can't be. I'm Aida. Call her friends and family and ask them," Heidi said.

They confirmed that she had been blind and that her name was indeed Aida.

The next day at the conference when another blind woman named Aida was healed, Heidi knew something was going on. It was not mere coincidence that the first three blind people who God healed all had her name.

She thought God was going to tell her she was an awesome, precious child, but that's not what He said to her at all.

When she asked God why the first three blind people He healed had her name, she felt the Lord saying it was because she was blind. She responded to the Lord that she was not blind; she was a missionary. But again she sensed Him saying she was blind.

Agreeing with Him was the only thing she knew to do, so she asked the Lord to explain this to her. She felt Him saying that she didn't see the Western first world or the Eastern first world. He spoke to her about seeing through the people's disguises to see how poor they really were. They were needy in different ways. Everyone needed love.

Heidi was happy in the bush; she was thrilled to be in Africa, not at all concerned with the Western world. More than anything she didn't understand how those in the West didn't, couldn't, and wouldn't see the poor.

Then she understood that she didn't see them, either.

They were poor and needy, but they were wearing disguises that masked the realities of their poverty. Their vision had grown so dim they could no longer understand real love because they had not seen it in action for such a long time. The church had failed them, and so had politics. Education hadn't helped either. Materialism certainly wasn't their answer, as the growing rate of clinical depression attested to.

Jesus wanted to use Heidi to show them what love really looked like.

It was only a few days later that Heidi received an unusual number of e-mails and invitations to speak in churches in the Western world. Usually she received an invitation once or twice a year, but this time the sheer number of invitations was astounding. It really did seem like God was speaking to her about this: He wanted her to see the rich as well as the poor.

———

At first Heidi wasn't happy about traveling and ministering internationally but when she realized how important it was, she committed one-third of her time to it.

When she spoke at conferences or churches in the developed world, she usually wore black, but in Mozambique, she dressed in bright, tropical colors—blues and greens that brought out the pure blue color of her eyes.

The first time I listened to Heidi preach in the Western world was at a multicultural, non-denominational church used to its own order and customs. When Heidi walked onto the platform, she was barefoot, and there was a sort of hushed surprise from those in the room who were members of the church.

They expected the usual, obligatory thirty-second prayer before she preached, but instead she prayed simply from her heart with great emotion and got down on her knees, her hands forming little cups in front of her. She prayed for ten, then fifteen, and then twenty minutes, until finally the people in the room stopped watching her and started praying themselves. When she finished praying, she spoke as she had prayed—simply and with heartfelt conviction.

Heidi was charismatic, funny, serious, piercing, and full of love, humility, and confidence all at the same time. The churchgoers were deeply moved when she spoke about her children who once were starving, abused, and neglected, living on the streets and in the dump, who had now found a home and family and were full of joy.

Heidi's main goal in every meeting—in every church service or conference—was to understand what the Holy Spirit wanted to say or do. Many times while traveling she would get off the plane, go directly to her hotel, and have just enough time to shower or change her clothes before she had to speak. Often she chose to pray, worship, and seek God about His purpose for the meeting instead of eating or showering.

She trusted that God knew what the people to whom she was speaking in any given meeting most needed. She was not traveling and speaking in order to raise money because she did not believe in formal fund-raising and had never asked for money. Rather, she wanted to give something meaningful, something of eternal value, to her listeners.

After she spoke, Heidi always gave the congregation a chance to respond. She encouraged people to be free and to do what they needed to do, and it was common for her to dismiss those who needed to leave early before she invited people to come forward for prayer ministry. Usually people came to the front to kneel or lie down, and they often wept. Sometimes

Heidi prayed during this time, but mostly she hugged people. She just held them while they cried their eyes out. "Blessed are those who mourn, for they shall be comforted" was one of Heidi's favorite scriptures. There was a lot of hidden pain and mourning in people's hearts, hidden sometimes even from themselves, but when Heidi hugged them and held them close as a mother comforts a child, the tears poured out, bringing light and healing into their dark places.

Some of the people who gathered around Heidi, hands raised, on their knees or prostrate on their faces, were so moved that they made plans to change something in their lives: to respond to her message by committing to stop for the one or to give their lives for others.

Many of them—easily a thousand people a year—visited Mozambique and the work there. When they visited Iris, they noticed how unique the ministry was. Somehow it wasn't institutionalized, even though it was an organization. It was an organic place, where a multitude of things happened at the same time. With people from all over the world living together in the same square mile, it was full of life and diversity and, as Rolland once said, Iris consisted of "people seeking to make their lives count."

Some of the visitors even gave up full-time careers in law or investment banking or business to do full-time missions work in Africa. Initially inspired by the Bakers, they soon also found themselves inspired by the nationals, creating bonds as strong as family ties with the Mozambicans they grew to know and love.

Over the years Heidi and Rolland realized the benefits of ministering cross-culturally and bringing people together from different parts of the world. The point was to create a kingdom culture, not a national identity, because the kingdom of heaven was filled with people who spoke every language ever known to man.

Heidi absolutely adored cultures and the differences in each one, and she had difficulty answering when I asked her which country she liked best.

"Oh, I like them all," she exclaimed.

"No, really. If you had to choose just one country, which would be your favorite to visit?"

"I really don't know. I so enjoy meeting the people and learning about their culture. I think the differences are just beautiful."

I didn't press her anymore. I got the feeling that it would be as hard for her to choose a favorite country as it would be for her to choose a favorite child. Parents were not supposed to have favorites, and around the world people looked to her for mentoring, spiritual guidance, and teaching. Now her speaking schedule was booked two years in advance with more invitations than she could possibly accept, and she was Mama Aida to people all over the world.

Chapter 15

EXPANSION

IN FEBRUARY 2000 a cyclone swept across southern Africa, creating severe floods across multiple countries. Mozambique was one of the hardest hit. There was no ark to save the people, and it took the Western world more than three weeks to respond. Many were stuck in trees or on rooftops for days without food or water as they watched the bloated bodies of animals and people float below them. One woman gave birth in a tree. There were just a handful of rescue helicopters to circle above the waters that displaced two million Mozambicans and killed almost one thousand.

The government told people to leave their houses because it wasn't safe to stay and the water would wash them away with their few earthly possessions. However, the government was not offering any shelter to the thousands of people who had nothing else to do but wander aimlessly away from the floodwater. Conditions for the displaced people became worse and worse. Corn that had been donated to feed the poor was being sold for profit, and a new school that had been built refused to open its doors to the refugees because they would ruin the school. People slept on the road and in gardens, hoping not to get bitten by malaria-carrying mosquitoes. Many died from a lack of available medicine.

Thieves attempted to steal what they could, even from the houses that were waterlogged. Even they were simply trying to survive. There was no drinking water available to anyone, and a bag of food, which would generally cost eight dollars, rose to almost fifty dollars—too much for the severely poor who had just lost everything to a natural disaster.

There were no social safety nets in Mozambique. Few developing countries could afford the luxury. The devastation of the tsunami in Indonesia cost insurance companies less than a Florida hurricane because fewer Asians could afford insurance.[1] Things like food and clean water in emergencies were the best things rural Mozambicans could hope for.

The United Nations called upon Heidi and Rolland and their organization to help provide emergency assistance to affected Mozambicans. Because Iris was one of the largest on-the-ground networks, Iris was more organized than any of the international organizations could be. As is common with nongovernmental organizations (NGOs), Iris had in-depth knowledge of the area as well as good relationships with the people and communities.

In this way Iris was prepared to offer food and emergency supplies. This type of service went back to what Heidi and Rolland learned in Asia: providing ministry that extended far beyond the spiritual, ministry that encompassed every aspect of life. In Heidi's words, "It's what love looked like." By serving people and helping them meet their most basic needs, Heidi and Rolland were demonstrating God's love and care.

During the floods Iris fed five thousand people in one day (in partnership with the UN) and eleven thousand the next day. The numbers kept increasing, and Iris found itself having access to the entire country. As they spread the word about the Bible schools they offered, young men and women flocked from their waterlogged villages to receive the Bible training and then eventually returned home to plant a new church. Explosive church growth occurred in this way, and Iris churches mushroomed into the thousands.

When asked about the physical healings Heidi now so often

sees in the bush of Mozambique, she replied that while physical healings were part of the whole, they were not the only part. She went on to define a love that is tangible—an action rather than words, an action that flows from compassion.

"If we just saw people who experienced physical miracles, it wouldn't make any sense at all," she said. "That would not be enough. It's about character, love for the dying, the sick, the broken. Compassion and mercy are God's heart. Miracles are fruit flowing out of intimacy with Him. The miracle of love has to be the central thing. We have people who are still blind and still crippled, but we can love them. It's about caring for people. We build them houses." And they helped in crises.

It seemed the floods and the country opening up to them were preparing them for something. As it turned out, God was preparing Heidi and Rolland to begin ministering in a very different part of Mozambique. After Heidi had been based in the capital city for a number of years, she heard God say, "Go get My Makua bride."

Heidi wasn't really sure who the Makua people were or where they were located or if they were even in Mozambique. She asked Rolland to find out where they were.

"I was so yielded at that point that if God showed up and told me to go to preach in Laguna Beach, I would have done it," Heidi told me. "But when He told me to go to the Makua, I was thinking, *How can I leave my children?* After all, she had 520 of them between Zimpeto and Machava, the two Iris centers in Maputo.

She heard God's reply loud and clear: "They're *My* children." Heidi needed to be reminded that He would care for them, and then it was easier for her to say, "Yes, Lord, I'll go."

Rolland discovered that the Makua were a people group

concentrated in the northern part of Mozambique. The closest town was Pemba, where there also happened to be a small airport. So they sent a scout north to meet the Makua, and a few months later, Heidi and Rolland visited Pemba for the first time. It was 2001.

During that initial visit Heidi preached on the street corner to twenty vendors who were all trying to sell her bead necklaces, chocolate bars, or little toy cars they had made. Heidi bought a few small things and invited them to a church service in a dirt field the following Saturday evening and Sunday morning. Heidi and Rolland's pastor friend, who happened to be visiting them in Mozambique for the first time, had come with them to Pemba, and they had asked him to preach.

But when the American pastor spoke to the people, none of them were listening. This was unusual because typically the fact that the preacher was an American would have been enough to draw a crowd. Though there was a crowd, the Mozambican men shouted and jeered, completely unreceptive to the pastor's words or message.

Sensing she should do something she had never done before, Heidi took the microphone that was powered by the small generator they had brought with them. She looked out at the small crowd, the whites of their eyes all she could see in the dark, and she wondered how to rebuke demons en masse. She didn't have the slightest clue how to do that.

Heidi believed there was a spiritual reality that superseded the material world. The Mozambicans certainly believed in the spiritual world. They were still visiting witch doctors for physical healing and supernatural power, praying to the gods who resided in massive baobab trees, and worshipping ancestors in cemeteries. As a Westerner it would take me a few years to come close to understanding how tightly the spiritual world is interwoven into everyday African life.

Heidi asked the crowd how many of them wanted to know God. When not one of them responded, she asked how many wanted to be free of demonic oppression. About thirty of them raised their hands. So she rebuked the demons and commanded them to go in the name of Jesus. Then she asked who wanted to know the love of God. Then everyone raised their hands.

After seeing the response and the great need, Heidi knew God had spoken to her about the Makua people, and as hard as it was to leave her kids, she and Rolland decided to relocate to Pemba. An Australian couple who had been serving with her for years would stay behind in Maputo to run the center and continue caring for the children.

Pemba was a three-hour flight from Maputo, and with the state of the roads it was almost impossible to drive there. Pemba was pretty desolate compared to Maputo. There were hardly any motorbikes or cars on the roads. Since Pemba was surrounded by water on three sides, there was only one direction to drive, and just a few miles out of town there was nothing but bush for hours and hours until the road finally forked in two. It would take a day or two to reach the next town.

The tropical temperatures, deep-blue sea, and green palm trees were certainly beautiful, but in the summer there were soaring temperatures with high humidity. Pemba had no running water and only sketchy electricity. Bright red dirt covered everything all the time, and the mosquitoes were numerous and carried malaria.

Nevertheless, Heidi was determined to make this new place home.

When they first moved north to Pemba, someone suggested to her that maybe God wanted her and Rolland to have a

house away from the children's center so she would be able to
have more time to herself, which really just meant more time
to spend alone with God. Living with hundreds of children
meant she and Rolland rarely had time to themselves.

But Heidi didn't think she could do that. Her past missions
philosophy of radical self-sacrifice was still so ingrained in her
that at first she could not imagine living even a mile away from
the center. Her whole identity had been as a missionary, and
she couldn't imagine living without the "radical, holy chaos"
of kids 24/7 and need and noise and her most important relationships. She couldn't understand anyone suggesting that she
have a little more space. For over twenty years she had lived in
the slums without any kind of fence or separation, because she
was taught that fences separated her from the poor.

Finally, after many others suggested the same thing, that it
would be good for them to have their own place, Heidi and
Rolland were willing to consider that maybe it would be beneficial for them to spend more time alone with Jesus, and they
started looking for their own home. Heidi found a small two-
bedroom house that she loved. It was located a little more than
a mile away from where the center would be. The only trouble
was that it wasn't for sale, and it didn't have water or electricity.

"It was no fancy schmancy, but it had a view that so delighted
my soul, as someone from Laguna, you know," Heidi said.
"God have mercy, I am a beach kid, and I didn't even know
there was a beach here in Pemba at first. At first, I said to God,
'I can't live in this pretty place.'"

"They're still lost in this pretty place, and I'm still drawing
you here," was how she heard God respond.

The man who owned the house told Heidi that it wasn't for
sale but that he was willing to sell her the bigger house behind
it if she wanted.

When Heidi expressed her desire to have a small house on

the water, the man responded: "I really don't want to sell my house." He paused thoughtfully. "But I'm going to sell it to you. My mother is terminally ill, and as soon as she dies, you can have it," he said.

Heidi had no money, but she knew from past experience with God that resources weren't a big deal to Him. If He wanted her to buy a house away from the center, then He would make it happen. She had learned long ago in her journey that she couldn't make decisions based on money; doing so actually made money into a god. Rather, when God said something, she learned to step out in faith, and then He always provided.

Just a few weeks later a church group from the United States came to visit Heidi and Rolland in Pemba and gave them a personal donation. Personal donations were rare, as most people gave to their ministry. With this donation the Bakers had enough to buy the house from the man who didn't really want to sell it.

As for the land where the new center would be built, that was a story too. Heidi felt silly even entertaining the thought that they could actually afford the land they wanted. It was a large, gorgeous piece of property, overgrown with foliage because no one was using it. The Indian man who owned it— and who also owned much of the land in the surrounding area—had recently built a fence around the property.

All the money Heidi and Rolland had amounted to less than 10 percent of the asking price. She drove through the property's dirt track, asking God if this really was the place. As she was driving, she saw a vision of her kids living here, and she grew confident that this land belonged to them, so she drove directly to town to meet with the owner, a man with whom she would later become friends.

Slightly embarrassed that she had so little money to offer, she entered his office, which was in the back of his shop. What she said was this: "I can give you 10 percent of the money right now, and within a year, I promise to pay you for all of it. No bank here is going to lend me the money unless I have the cash up front to show them."

"All right, I will sell you the land," he said with a slight smile on his face. Though he had a gentle voice, he had a reputation as a shrewd businessman. She could hardly believe that he had agreed! There were no lawyers involved. They drafted a document together and signed it. He gave her all the documents to the land, and the even bigger miracle was that within three months, she was able to pay it off in cash.

Not long after the land was completely paid for, the former owner realized its real value and offered to buy it back for double the price. Heidi graciously declined.

Shortly after she purchased the land, Pastor Miguel, one of the Iris pastors in Pemba, told her that the land had been used for idol worship. Many villagers had journeyed to the massive baobab trees to make sacrifices to the gods who they believed lived in the trees.

Pastor Miguel once found a bright red piece of fabric (called a *capulana*) nailed to the tree and underneath there was a small plate with coins and a baby chick nearby. He told his wife, "Let's take this stuff to use at home."

"No we can't; bad things will happen to us because of the spirits in the trees," she said.

"Nothing will happen to us," he replied confidently while gathering up the offerings to take them home. When the chick grew up and had its own chicks, Pastor Miguel brought the chicken to the Iris church as an offering.

On the tenth anniversary of Heidi buying the land in Pemba, she and her Western and Mozambican staff were having a staff meeting and celebrating all that had happened in the last decade. Iris had gone from Heidi and Rolland Baker's personal ministry to an international mission organization that had bases, children's centers, and churches in dozens of countries.

One thing that was strong on Heidi's heart was the racism the Mozambicans had encountered for many years throughout their history. "We are so sorry for the way people treated you," she told the Mozambican leaders and pastors. "You are so valued. Thank you for the ways you help us make this our home too. We love you so much."

The missionaries and Heidi formed a circle around the Mozambicans then, asking Jesus for His blessing on these beloved brothers and sisters in front of them, that He would raise up their country, bowed down from poverty and oppression, and that destiny and purpose would rise like a phoenix rising from the ashes.

Chapter 16

POLITICAL CRISIS

W HEN HEIDI RECEIVED a phone call from her businessman friend who sold her the land in Pemba, her
first thought was, "It's Saturday. I just want a day off.
I need to be alone." Heidi enjoyed solitude, but you'd never
know it with all the people constantly surrounding her, even
sometimes lining up in the driveway outside her Pemba house.

He was calling to tell her about an article in the newspaper
that accused Heidi Baker and her senior Iris staff of being
against the government, saying they left "like lightning" in
planes and buses when the government office tried to contact
them about their political stance, as if their leaving was proof
they were guilty.

They *had* left Pemba, but not because of any opposition to
the government. They hadn't even known about the accusation
when they left for their staff retreat, a meeting of 160 of their
senior staff from various bases, in the south of Mozambique,
near Maputo.

The news that Iris was against the current government party
was displayed on the *African Times* website and even broad-
cast on the news on television in Maputo. An article was also
printed in the local paper: the title read, "Heidi Baker, Director
of Iris, Is Contra-Government." There was also an accusation that she supported the opposition party. These accusations brought back flashbacks of having their entire center in
Maputo, including the fifty-five buildings they had renovated

with Iris finances, confiscated. The civil war had raged for seventeen years, and the tensions were not easily forgotten.

Soon after the article was published, Heidi started receiving death threats on her cell phone. No one knew from whom the text messages were coming. Were they coming from some of the Makua men from the community who believed Heidi preferred the Shangaan, a tribe from the south? Or perhaps they were from someone who believed there were individuals inside Iris who were involved in politics. Heidi pointed out that the highest paid workers at the center were the teachers of the recently opened primary school, who were men and women from the Makua tribe. But still, four or five times a day, she received a text that said, "We are going to kill you."

Her Shangaana sons were receiving the same messages, which led her to believe the culprit was someone from the local area. Other Mozambican groups often resented the Shangaana tribe due to their privilege. Because the Shangaana were from the capital city, they had control of the resources and consequently the education and power.

The article's accusations had created problems with the government that, in the midst of the death threats, Heidi had to sort out quickly. There were also problems at the primary school, but she needed to address the situation with the government first, or there might not be a school. The government had the power to kick Iris out of the country, which was the way things seemed to be heading now that they thought Iris did not support the current government. Heidi even heard a rumor that the government officials thought she and Rolland might be spies. In her mind it was absurd, but this was a foreign system that operated much differently than any government system in the West.

"You can imagine how I feel," Heidi told me. "The last time

they did this, they took away fifty-five buildings; they beat my kids. And on top of it all, I had malaria."

Heidi called the editor who had written the article: "How can you be so irresponsible with your journalism? There's not a fact in that article. You spelled my name right; that's about it. How can you be so inaccurate? This is not responsible journalism."

"I'll get back to you," he said. Meanwhile, he stood by his story when he spoke with the president of Mozambique, telling him Heidi did not support the government. The president responded by sending the social justice department to investigate.

One Monday morning Heidi visited the office of the man who wrote the article, but she was not allowed inside to speak with anyone. She spent two days in the tiny front office, where the humidity was causing the paint to peel off the walls. She was waiting to speak to someone—anyone—but no one would talk to her.

On Wednesday she returned again to the government office with a pastor-friend who led a church in Pemba. That day the government building was not surrounded by guards holding guns, as it usually was, nor was there a receptionist present.

"They're gone; we can go in," she said smiling somewhat mischievously and clapping her hands in front of her, knowing this was her opportunity to speak to someone.

"We can't do that," the pastor said gravely. She thought she could detect him turning pale.

"I'm going. You can come or you can stay. It's my opportunity. I have to go," she said.

"It's really, really dangerous," he said, looking at her, knowing by now that nothing he said would dissuade her. "Oh, God," the pastor said as he started praying, loudly, as they walked past the empty desk of the receptionist.

Heidi shushed him.

At the top of the staircase they ran directly into the author of the article.

"How did you get in?" he demanded.

"Hi, how are you? I'm so happy to talk to you," she said in Portuguese. "We just came up the stairs, sir. I want to talk you about the article in the newspaper."

"How did you get in here?" he demanded again.

"There was no one around, so we just walked up the steps. I'm not leaving, sir, until someone speaks to me."

He glared at her. "Sit there," he said, pointing to a chair in an empty office, where he left her for almost an hour. The office was barren. There were no photos or pictures hung; it was just four concrete walls.

When he finally returned, he sat down across from her. His eyes narrowed. "I don't want to talk to you," he said. "You're against the government."

"No..." Heidi couldn't stop the tears then, those same feelings of helplessness resurfacing from years ago when the government had taken the children's center in Maputo. "I just want to love God and love children."

He spoke then, listing all of the reasons he believed she was contra-government. Heidi listened sympathetically, nodding her head as he spoke.

When he finished, she addressed his concerns. "I'm here to bless you, not to hurt you. I'm just a simple woman in the dirt loving children. I promise I'm not against the government. I am not involved in politics here at all. The only reason I came is to love. Maybe I don't always do it well, but that's my job and it's what I try to do."

They went back and forth for at least an hour. Heidi was desperate for him to understand her heart and motives. She really tried to be apolitical. Iris was a nongovernmental organization.

It was based in the United States, and their primary objective was to care for vulnerable children.

When the writer put his hand over his heart, Heidi could see that his facial features had softened. "This is a beautiful day," he said. "My heart was in knots, and I was sick to my stomach because I believed you were trying to take down my government." He paused, no longer glaring at her, but instead looking intently into her eyes. "But now I have found the truth, and I will write another article. It will be on the front page, and I'll rescind every comment. I'll also speak to the president. But you should know that there are some people in your organization who are part of the opposition party."

"If that is so, I will find them and speak to them. We are not political, but we support your party because you want to help the poor too. We believe in honoring the government, and we pray for the president," Heidi replied. She was relieved. "We want to work together with you, and it hurts when people write things about me that aren't true." For a well-educated woman she had the ability to speak simply to make herself understood, the way a child does by emphasizing emotion rather than logic.

The leader looked at the blonde American woman in front of him, still in tears. "I believe you," he said. "And we will write an article of apology. We will work together."

"I'm so relieved," Heidi said. "Thank you. We would like to invite you to come share with the students at our cultural school next week. We would be honored." Heidi called the missions school a cultural school, not knowing if the government officials understood the concept of missions.

He extended his hand toward her.

The following week the controversy continued at the Iris staff meeting in Pemba. A day before the governor and his staff were to visit the cultural school, two Mozambican Bible school students were at an impasse. Armando was accusing Jorge of organizing the political resistance; Jorge had also been accused of immorality in the anonymous text messages.

Unlike Armando, Jorge had an education and was a man who wore his dignity like a cloak around him. He walked stiffly, upright, his chest pushed out in front of him as if he had once been in the military. Jorge had the ability to articulate his thoughts and speak logically. Armando, on the other hand, had difficulty communicating clearly.

Heidi questioned Armando about events he and Jorge disagreed on. "How do you know what happened?" Heidi asked.

"I have a computer in my head. I remember things," Armando said.

"He has a computer in his head," Heidi repeated doubtfully.

It was clear Heidi thought Jorge was more credible. She had been trying for weeks to sort out the dispute between the men on her own. As far as she could see, they weren't getting anywhere, so she decided to discuss the conflict with some of the staff. "If it can't be resolved here, we'll have to take it before the church," she said.

The staff members, myself included, sat in a bare concrete room with large cutouts for windows, the strong breeze kicking up dust, the long row of children's dormitories behind us, the burnt-orange color of the buildings blending in with the landscape. Hard wooden benches formed a sort of circle so that we looked at each other. Jorge sat directly to Heidi's right. Armando sat a few feet away from Jorge. Armando seemed a bit intimidated by the whole situation, blinking often and refusing to look at Jorge.

"This is not a game," Heidi said to the Western staff. "You might think it doesn't matter, that it's just a political party, but people have killed each other for years over this—killed each other! And I'm getting death threats. Eight more of them just today. I just get tired, you know. I can't bear this burden on my own, so that's why I'm letting you in on this..."

Someone asked if the calls were traceable.

"No," she replied. "They buy new phone SIM cards downtown, so there's no way to tell who it is. They're cowards. They won't come talk to me. I've invited them into my office to talk to me in person, but they won't."

There was a debate in the world of international development about the political nature of humanitarian aid. The conclusion was that, of course, the type of aid Iris gave to Mozambicans had political ramifications. However, the minimalists argued that saving lives was the most important agenda, regardless of politics. It was into this camp that Iris fell.

When Heidi asked Jorge if he was part of the opposition party, he replied with an adamant, "No." Everything was on the line for these two men—their positions at the school and their reputations in the community.

After an hour-and-a-half meeting, Heidi stopped the conversation, saying it was too painful and tedious to make us sit and listen any longer, that they would continue in her office. Before they left, she asked the Westerners to pray for the Mozambicans. As the staff prayed for Jorge, he got down on his knees, his face to the ground, and he wept, loud, unashamed sobs that echoed off the concrete floor.

The following week, when I traveled with one of the long-term missionaries to Nampula, the province south of Pemba, we were given the task of buying a new motorbike for Jorge, and we returned to the news that Armando had visited a witch doctor and was now acting crazy.

A few days later Armando was on the concrete porch outside of Heidi's office with a small group of pastors from the Bible school surrounding him. Heidi sat beside him, with her hand on his as she affirmed him in Portuguese.

"Precious son, we love you," Heidi said. "*Nos amamos.* We bless you, your house, *tudo*, everything. Love conquers hurt and fear." The Mozambican pastors also held his hands and prayed quietly.

Heidi began to sing over him, as if she were singing to one of her children who had a bad dream. "*Jesus ficando por aqui.*" She changed the song from "Jesus pass by here" to "Jesus stay here." The pastors accompanied her solo soprano voice in perfect a cappella.

This scene came after Armando had physically struck Jorge in the middle of another meeting in Heidi's office. When Armando had started ranting incoherently, the words just barely recognizable enough for Heidi to understand, Heidi recognized some of the same phrases that had been in the death threats.

When Armando started running around like a madman, Heidi acted quickly and decided to move the meeting outside to pray for Armando. Eventually he repented for his visits to the witch doctor, seeming genuinely sorry, and later lay still on the ground as Heidi sang over him.

When she finished singing to Armando, Heidi told the pastors to stay and pray over him. She had another meeting.

Power was a heady thing. Going to Bible school and becoming a pastor was one way to better yourself, one way to gain position. Visiting a witch doctor was another way, an attempt by some to gain more power. Heidi's message to the Mozambican Bible school students was not one of power and prestige but one of humility, of taking the lowest place in order to love others and to prefer them.

She spoke the same message to her staff of Westerners. They were there to educate the Mozambicans, to empower them, and to work themselves out of a job. They were to serve their brothers and sisters. "Going low" and serving was the only true way to love, and for Heidi, it was always about love and only love.

———————————

The next day there was a sort of low-intensity frenzy in the missions school. At Heidi's invitation the government officials were coming to speak.

Over the years the Bakers had welcomed everyone to visit their ministry and participate in their work in Mozambique. In more recent years they had set up even better structures like the missions school to encourage visitors to come, learn, and experience the mission field. The students of the first missions school faced harsh conditions: spotty electricity, no running water, and no real bathrooms. In fact, they had to dig through the hard ground to build their own latrines. Some students, unable to adjust to the rough conditions, left for home after only the first week or two. Others stayed, toughing it out.

The two hundred Western missions school students were aware of the accusations against Iris and Heidi's subsequent follow-up meeting, and the students buzzed around the compound, picking up trash and tidying the chairs to prepare for the officials' visit. This was part of their class time—learning to be content doing things no one else wanted to do, learning to serve. True humanitarian work looked like this: helping the human family climb the economic and social ladders even if it meant you took one step down. It might also mean giving up some luxuries so someone else could have some necessities.

When the government representatives finally arrived, driving past the green-and-white circus-sized tent where the students had their classes, the tension could be felt. What would they say? Were they actually going to speak? Would there be trouble? Heidi knew they still had the power to take all of this away, to close the school and send everyone home.

Heidi welcomed them, striding up to the six men in the long, graceful strides of a former dancer. She extended her hands in greeting, welcoming them in her effusive way. "Welcome to our school," she said, beaming, her energetic and warm welcome not showing them the nervousness just underneath.

The men were very formal. They wore starched blue dress shirts, trousers with black leather belts, and thick leather shoes that any of the Mozambican pastors would covet. The students were mostly wearing shorts and T-shirts, the female students in long skirts and T-shirts.

The students in the missions school had come from all over the world, and Heidi hoped that by introducing the various countries, the officials would feel honored that all of these people had come to Mozambique. "Welcome, Germany," Heidi said, proceeding through the list of countries and tribes. "England," she called out, and the students hollered and shouted. The students were fully participating, as they continued to welcome students from each nation. "Brazil!" Another shout went up. Then on to the African countries: Sudan, Sierra Leone, Malawi, South Africa. Then the Mozambican tribes: Makua, Maconde, Shangaan.

There were lots of cheers for Canada and the United States, which were home to the majority of students. There were also students from Australia, New Zealand, France, Hong Kong, Indonesia, China, South Korea; it was a long list, and there were many greetings, everyone seemingly caught up in the joy of diversity. Even the government officials started to smile. Their faces began to show signs of softening.

The main speaker took the microphone, greeting everyone

in all of the languages he knew. He was smiling. When no one responded to his greeting in Swahili, he was surprised, laughing and teasing the people.

Then he began in Portuguese: "Our party is in charge. We're preparing for Congress in November."

I wondered if he was going to tell us what to believe about the country. Would he use this as a political platform?

He continued: "We're looking for keys to help our country. In our party, we have teachers, educators taking care of children, carpenters, many people doing different jobs. There are many Mozambicans here, and they should know what's going on in our country."

And then he changed key, as he seemed to know his audience and was willing to try to relate. "I'm not a practicer of religion, and I don't know deep religious things, but I pray, and I know that everything that is of love is from God, that loving others comes from God."

Soon he was almost preaching, this man who was not religious.

"The children when they find you, they find love and find someone to take care of them. Maybe one day my children will need this love that you're studying here. I wish you the best studies. Thank you for your work and for wanting to learn how to reach the world with love. *Obrigado,*" he said, ending with "thank you" in Portuguese.

The men seemed to enjoy being the center of affectionate attention, and they left with smiles and much fanfare. They said good-bye to Heidi by kissing her on both cheeks and shaking her hands. Some of the older American women in the school ran up to shake their hands, the way they would if the president of the United States had visited.

The students had, in fact, just received a visit from representatives of the president of Mozambique, and it had gone well.

The crisis was averted, and instead of reprimanding Iris, the officials thanked them for their humanitarian work and for their love in practice. These students were the ones who were learning from Heidi and Rolland, and they would endeavor to take this practical love around the world.

Chapter 17

THE IRIS FAMILY

FOR THE FIRST ten years or so in Pemba, Iva, one of Heidi's grown adopted daughters, was the director of the children's center there. Heidi brought Iva with her when she first moved to Pemba from Maputo. When Iva was a child, she lived in the children's center in Maputo and was there when Heidi first took it over from the government.

The children's center was a fitting name for a place where the carefree children looked plump and healthy from three meals a day and where they enjoyed growing up with many brothers and sisters, mothers and fathers, and aunts and uncles. Compared to the rest of Mozambique's children, they had unique opportunities that came from living in such an international community.

Some of the local village kids often claimed they were orphans or abandoned because they wanted the same benefits of living in the Iris children's center. The village kids were always at the Iris church and playground because they desired to be part of the large family too, where there was no worry about having enough food for the day.

Iva, once one of these children, was now a strong young woman. She had the ability to empathize with the kids because she knew firsthand what it felt like to lose both of her parents. She was only six when they died: first her mother from a stomach infection and then her father in the same year. Afterward her aunt took in Iva and her siblings.

"My aunt didn't like us," Iva said, remembering the past

with a grimace on her face, her dark-brown eyes solemn as she looked at me and then down at her print dress. "She hated us."

After only a short time her aunt abandoned them, leaving them at the government-run children's center in the south of Mozambique. Iva particularly remembered the food there. "It was very bad, but it was better than eating the garbage we had to eat when my aunt didn't feed us. The center was terrible."

Her round face softened as she remembered what happened next. The first candy she ever tasted in her life came from a white woman who began visiting the children's center. Iva was fourteen when the government gave the center to the American woman Iva now calls Mama Aida.

Iva, then a sad, shy, malnourished girl with a bloated belly and very short brown hair, distinctly remembered Heidi and Rolland's arrival. It was the start of her new life. At the memory of the Bakers' arrival, Iva smiled slightly, and her eyes seemed to brighten. She started talking freely then, and I was no longer interviewing her.

> Mama Aida talked to us about Jesus, and I understood I'm not alone; there's someone who really loves me. I started to become happy. Before that I felt totally alone, like there was no hope in the world. When my aunt left us, she never visited us again. It was like she threw out the trash. Even when the government-run children's center had meetings for extended family, she wouldn't come.
>
> After I met Jesus, I met Celio. I was fifteen. I didn't meet him because I wanted to. I was still suffering. But it was a way to overcome some of my loneliness. Then when I became pregnant, I suffered even more. Celio decided he wanted to marry another girl instead, so he beat me then sent me away. I cried so much. I thought it was better to die, and I tried to kill myself. I stole

cleansing solution from the hospital and was going to
drink it. Mama Aida found me and ripped the poison
out of my hand.

[Then Celio returned and] I got pregnant again. Celio
was drinking, smoking, using drugs. I didn't want to
give up on him because I loved him. I loved my kids.
All I knew how to do was pray. I prayed for Celio, and
Mama Aida stood with me. She taught me how to be
strong and courageous. We prayed together so often. I
thank God that He brought this strong woman to our
nation.

Mama Aida got Celio a job in the city doing various
tasks, and slowly he began to change. It took seven years
for him to turn his life around, but he has changed so
much. He doesn't smoke or drink or use drugs or see
other women. Celio loves Jesus, and now he works with
me helping children.

Together our dream is that the kids will grow up here
happy and become preachers, presidents, ministers, and
professors who will fight for our nation of Mozambique.
We want to fight for the nation of Mozambique, for
every abandoned child in Mozambique, that they too
would be loved. I don't want anyone else to go through
what I did, and I know Jesus has even more to do in my
life. These kids are the future of Mozambique.[1]

When Iva became pregnant at fifteen, she had to quit
school, but because she had always enjoyed school, she
was returning to finish her degree. After working all day
at the center, she attended evening classes. Dressed in
a long black skirt and pink dress shirt, and holding a
black hat, Iva was on her way to school. As she centered
the hat on her head, she told me in English, with a wide
grin, "Michael Jackson!" She spun once, imitating him,
and giggled like a girl.

Heidi watched Iva with a big smile: *"Um beijo* (a kiss)," she told Iva before she left for school. They kissed each other, Mozambican-style, on both cheeks. Strong, courageous, and determined, Iva was very much like her Mama Aida, unwilling to let her culture's treatment of women keep her down. As Heidi had once shown her, Iva showed the children they were not alone, that there was someone who cared for them with a mother's love that was as sweet as the candy Iva had first tasted over two decades ago.

Relationships were the most important part of life in Mozambique, and the people were the ones who made Iris what it is today. The Iris base in Pemba consisted of two hundred or so kids who lived on base and who were adopted into the Iris family, fifty or so missionaries, the Mozambican staff, and thousands of Mozambican villagers who lived nearby. For five months out of the year, there were also the Mozambican Bible school students as well as the missions school students.

After finishing the two-month missions school, some of the students came back to work with Iris full time and become missionaries. In order to make Mozambique their home, they had to give up their steady incomes, comfortable houses, and quality time with family and friends to live in Pemba, the place that sometimes felt like the end of the earth.

Jeff and Janet Tarbill attended the first session of the school, leaving behind their home near Seattle, Washington. Janet was a library technician, and Jeff was a builder who designed and built hand-crafted staircases and worked on high-end custom houses. They had recently finished building their own dream home and often invited friends to stay with them in the guest bedroom, where they spoiled them with small luxuries.

Their life was comfortable and fun; their two children were

both in their twenties. Even though the Tarbills finally had what they had worked so hard for, they felt something was missing. The American dream had not been as fulfilling as they thought it would be. One day Jeff walked into the living room to find Janet and declared that if this was all there was, God could just take him now. He wasn't finding joy in the same old things.

A few months later they attended a conference where Heidi was speaking. At the end of her talk she called for those who wanted to be missionaries. Many rushed to the front to accept the call and ask her to pray for them. When Janet looked around and couldn't find Jeff, she asked her friends if they had seen him. They hadn't.

"Surely he wouldn't be up there," she said. Then she saw him in the crowd—he was at the front. She rushed to him immediately. When Heidi finished praying for him, Janet said, "We have to talk about why you're up here." She didn't want to be a missionary.

"Yeah," he said. "I really felt the Holy Spirit tell me to come up here. I don't know why, but I just want to obey Him." He spoke gently and slowly, as he usually did.

Janet was almost frantic by now. She went over to where Heidi was sitting and said, "I have to ask you something. You talked about being a missionary but I have a Bible study in my home and have led some women to God. I don't want to go anywhere else."

"What you are doing is missions," Heidi replied. "Sure, you can do missions in your home. But the conundrum of the gospel is that if you try to save your life you will lose it and if you lose it you will save it."

The words haunted Janet.

Jeff was certain when they got home. "I want to sell the house and move to Africa."

She was horrified. Really? He wanted them to quit their jobs and leave their children and their country? They were already in their late fifties. Wasn't it too late to start over?

But underneath there was just the faintest twinge of excitement, and within twenty-four hours it would blossom until Janet was convinced moving to Africa would be an adventure she wanted to take.

When she talked to her friends about the possibility of becoming a missionary, they were shocked. A few of them said she and Jeff weren't hearing from God at all. "How could you leave your children?" they asked. "You can't sell your house," others said. Though it was painful to hear these things from some of their friends, in just a few days Janet and Jeff were both convinced. They would sell the house. Only months later they were on their way to Mozambique, and their daughter would take care of the final details on the sale of their estate.

In Mozambique they bought a small house close to the ocean, near Heidi and Rolland's property. Jeff remodeled it so that it looked like a cottage from a Thomas Kinkade painting. They spent five years in their Mozambican home, and then they rented it out and were sent as ambassadors of joy to another Iris base in central Mozambique for three months. Their easygoing and laid-back personalities were needed to lighten up the atmosphere in Beira, where the missionaries had just gone through some relational difficulties. Jeff and Janet went to throw some parties and create some adventure or maybe plan a trip to Victoria Falls in Zimbabwe or something.

They still did not fit the profile of missionaries. Janet's daughter's coworker was shocked when he met Janet for the first time. Taking note of Janet's fashionable clothes and stylish blonde hair, he exclaimed, "But you don't look like a missionary!"

In Mozambique, Jeff and Janet learned to value relationships and love their neighbors in a new way.

Each Iris missionary had a remarkable story worthy of being told; each story was unique, but they all shared this commonality: the individuals had left their home countries and everything familiar and comfortable to serve the extremely poor as if they were kings and queens.

Some of the missionaries worked in the kitchen, helping the Mozambican staff. The kitchen job was one of the most challenging roles on the base. Some of the workers continually stole food and sometimes even cleaning supplies. The theft was constant, and it was hard to address it without damaging relationships, which were even more crucial while laying the foundations of the ministry. If the people didn't receive the missionaries, there was no point in being there.

Not long after the Pemba base started, a man came from Maputo to work in the ministry. Rumor was he had murdered someone. One of the Mozambican leaders wept bitterly when he heard the man was coming to work at Iris and thought this was just one more example of Heidi's deep and seemingly unending capacity for mercy. The rumor was only known among the Mozambicans, and no one knew if he had really committed murder. Heidi wasn't aware of the rumor.

A year and a half after the man started, he was fired for stabbing a coworker at the Pemba base. When Heidi fired him, he went crazy with anger, and he confronted her in her office, screaming and threatening her. When she finally left the center, the man was waiting for her at her house. Heidi drove away quickly and booked a room at the resort hotel to make sure she'd be safe since Rolland was traveling at the time.

Some of the missionaries were relieved to see the man go. They had known from the beginning that he was the wrong person for the job, but this was a place of grace, and Heidi often couldn't resist bringing the most challenging ones home with her. Some of the youth who had been kicked out of the center in Maputo were now living in Pemba. One used to steal cars for a living, and now he was in charge of the transportation department. Another adopted son had run away nine times. He always came home, knowing he would have a place with Mama Aida.

This young man was doing so much better; he knew he was loved even in the midst of his wrong decisions and anger problems. Most likely he had something like bipolar disorder, but the love and constancy had helped him so he was more mellow and more responsible for his actions. There would always be an ongoing debate among the missionaries and Mozambicans who worked with Heidi about the merits or pitfalls of these grace-filled decisions.

At times the cultures of the Westerners and the Mozambicans came together in interesting ways, another result of having such a multicultural organization like Iris.

Two of the missionaries, who were married and had been serving in Pemba for three years, were having a baby.

Susie was just entering her ninth month of pregnancy, and her slight, petite body was transformed by the balloon-like stomach she carried low. The original plan had been to travel to South Africa or back to her husband's home in the States to deliver the baby, but somehow that plan had come and gone, as many things do in African time. She was in no rush, but then it was too late for her to travel. She kind of knew she was letting time pass. There would be a doctor in the missions school until August 2 and Susie really hoped the baby would come early so she wouldn't have to deliver in the small, bush hospital in town.

On the day of the baby shower a plain, open-air room was transformed by huge bouquets of bougainvillea with their bright pink and resplendent purple blooms. There were two tables brimming with food unlike the Mozambicans had ever seen—traditional baby shower food: egg salad sandwiches cut into dainty triangles, tuna salad, sliced tomatoes, quiche, cinnamon rolls, fruit salad, and a huge chocolate cake.

The Mozambicans were on one side of the room in their traditional *capulanas*, a type of sarong, and head wraps. Many of the women had their children with them and sat on the floor. The other guests, mostly Westerners and mostly white, were on the other side of the room.

Because of the language barrier the Mozambicans and Westerners each talked amongst themselves. Heidi arrived thirty minutes late, dressed in a simple, form-fitting black dress. She did not announce her arrival in any way. Someone who didn't know Heidi might think she was sometimes shy. Gracious would be a more fitting description. Heidi calls herself an introvert.

Heidi first hugged her own daughter Crystalyn, who was visiting from the United States, and then she wandered over to the corner to greet everyone with hugs. She got a small plate of food and sat to eat beside Crystalyn, who had her mother's bright blue eyes and blonde hair, though hers was long and wavy. Before long Heidi was sitting on the floor beside the Mozambican women deep in conversation, her black dress already dirty with the dust she sat in. The effort of holding the conversation with ten or fifteen women was evident by the sweat that dripped down the side of her face. Her hair was slightly damp from perspiration, but she was smiling.

The guests were aware of her presence the way one is aware of the presence of a celebrity, though she stopped to greet and hug each one. The Mozambican women were enamored with her. The hostess of the party, an American missionary, announced that it was time to share a piece of advice or a story with Susie. The Mozambican women let it be known that in their culture, at this time the single women would leave the room, but Heidi said, "We're sharing culture today," so no one had to leave.

The first woman to speak was Mozambican, and she moved to sit beside Susie so she could look into her eyes. She was not speaking to the larger group of women, and her voice was soft. Heidi sat at their feet and translated for those who didn't speak Portuguese. Some of the advice Susie received sounded outlandish to the women from other cultures. "Don't wear pants or underwear from this moment on"; "No hot water from today forward. If you drink hot water the baby will bleed"; "Try not to breathe too hard"; and finally, "When you take a shower, don't put water on your head. If water touches your hair, you'll become bald, and the hair will fall out from left to right."

"What position do you assume when in childbirth?" someone asked the Mozambicans. One of the women, a mother of ten children, sat on the floor, legs open, and demonstrated how she would give birth if she were alone. She positioned herself in front of a chair or something she could hold onto and braced herself while she pushed, holding her breath, her face clenched tight. The woman let out a popping, spewing sound as she made the gesture of a baby flying out. Everyone roared with laughter, especially the Mozambicans.

If the Mozambican woman in labor had family, her mother or sister would act as a midwife and would stand above the mother-to-be, grasping her around the shoulders while the mother-to-be grabbed the back of the woman's legs, pushed, and delivered.

The acting midwife would clean the baby and then push on

the woman's stomach to clean her out. In the hospital, they said, the doctor pulled it all out at once, making a face that told everyone that having a baby in the hospital was even more painful. Mozambican women made little noise during childbirth and did not cry.

Three or four of the Mozambican women were currently pregnant; one of them was sixteen. Mozambicans typically had many children and wanted as many as possible because the mortality rate was so high that many of their babies would not make it past five years old. Children were also the only insurance policy they had. When they were old, they would need someone to care for them.

The other women told Heidi that traditionally when someone from the Makua tribe gave baby advice, the expectant mother put coins in her hands as a sort of payment, but because they were Christians they wouldn't ask for money.

"Thank you," Susie responded, laughing.

Heidi was still on the floor, now in the middle of the two groups of women, her tan legs crossed gracefully in front of her. Bridging the gap, she translated and sometimes laughed at the differences among the various cultures. "Don't wash your hair," she repeated smiling, "or you'll go bald."

Heidi seemed so far removed from her own culture that she didn't even think to tell the Mozambican women that Westerners didn't lose their hair. Heidi, who spoke eight languages and had lived all over the world, embraced many cultures as her own. The bleached-blonde hair only hinted at the California beach culture to which she once belonged. It was as if she had become the literal bridge.

Chapter 18

WOMEN WERE MADE
IN GOD'S IMAGE TOO

A T FIRST ZAMIRA was afraid of us, without reason of course, but still, she was afraid. Zamira lived in the nearby Pemba village, and her circumstances were similar to those of millions of Mozambican women.

When Zamira's husband died, she moved to Pemba, hoping she could find work to support her children. She found a job washing laundry and cleaning the house of an Iris missionary. When the missionary returned to the United States, my husband and I were back in Mozambique living on the Pemba base and agreed to let Zamira come by to help us with chores at our house.

Zamira kept to herself, and for the first month she rarely spoke to us. She worked so hard in the brilliant African sun that large droplets of sweat beaded on her forehead and soaked through her apron. Washing laundry by hand was the only way to wash clothes in Africa, so Zamira filled brightly colored plastic buckets with cold water that she pumped out of the well. Scrubbing the burnt orange dirt out of our clothes was tedious work, and washing by hand meant something entirely different in Mozambique than in the States. The clothes were scrubbed vigorously and then thoroughly wringed until they no longer dripped when squeezed. Hand washing and line drying in the tropical sunshine meant that within weeks or months, the clothes were misshapen and discolored.

We tried to make conversation with Zamira. She answered

respectfully and politely but scurried out of our presence as soon as she could, her head tucked down as she looked at her feet, making her seem even shorter than her five-foot frame.

I realized that she had probably heard the widely circulated stories about *acunas*, the white people: "They captured our people in nets and made them prisoners in their forts. Then they loaded them into ships and took them away across the sea." Or perhaps, "*Acunas* came and took our land. They stole our resources. They are greedy for gold and diamonds." Or even worse, "*Acunas* will steal your children; they will sell them for their organs." Her country had been colonized for five hundred years, and these were the stories of their past.

Zamira was born in the Mozambican bush in a mud hut surrounded by twenty or so other mud huts. The frames of the houses were built with bamboo. The holes were filled in with rocks and mud, and the roof was nothing more than dried grass. Some of the huts were sturdily built; some were falling apart. A few of the dwellings had many holes in the walls, the sunlight piercing through the rocks and mud to shine light into the dark, cool rooms, but at night the holes were open entrances for disease-carrying mosquitoes.

Each day was like the last; time was as fluid as the river from which they got their drinking water. Time was marked not by clocks or watches but by the sun because without electricity, there was nothing to do during the night. If a person was fortunate, he or she could afford a small kerosene lantern to slow the encroaching darkness.

Zamira didn't know how old she was when I met her. She looked like she was around forty, but because of the hardships of daily living, most adults looked older than they were. The average Mozambican life expectancy was fifty-three.[1]

When I asked Zamira how old her children were, she shrugged her shoulders and made a hand gesture to indicate how tall they were, confident this was sufficient to explain their ages. By American standards Mozambican children typically appeared to be two years younger than their age because of malnutrition. Zamira's oldest child was a girl named Katarina, who was around eleven years old; the youngest looked to be about three.

They were from the Makua tribe, and the Makua language was oral, not written. Though Zamira had never attended school and couldn't read or write, she was extremely dignified. When she enrolled her daughter in primary school, she couldn't sign her name on the enrollment form. She bore the shame by thinking about the better life education would create for her firstborn. In turn Katarina taught her mother Portuguese, the national language of Mozambique, and how to sign her name.

One afternoon I sat down at the kitchen table for a short lunch and a break from the burning sun and heavy demands of the day. While I ate, I turned on a film about Mother Teresa that a friend had lent me. On days like this one when nothing went the way I hoped, when I spent three hours trying to send an e-mail or print a document or four hours grocery shopping in the noisy and cluttered market stalls, I needed inspiration and a reminder of why I was in Mozambique in the first place. When things were difficult, it was easy to want to return to the comforts of the first world.

Zamira was at our house that day washing dishes at the kitchen sink when I noticed her looking over her shoulder. As the sound and images of poor Kolkata (formerly Calcutta) flickered from my computer, she left the sink to stare. Her dark eyes narrowed in surprise. I watched her closely, noticing that she reacted as if she had never before seen a film. Her mouth hung slightly open in disbelief.

"Where is this?" she asked me.

"India," I replied, not sure if she had ever heard of India.

"Oh..." Her voice trailed off as she stood rooted to the floor, silently absorbing the images of the beggar children in dirty rags, the pollution of the big city, an old feeble man lying in the middle of the sidewalk, and the woman in a blue dress who noticed him as she walked by to catch her bus, stopping suddenly to reach down and touch him. Zamira was riveted as she watched the woman struggle internally, looking first at the arriving bus and then down at the man, and Zamira uttered a small cry when the woman chose to let the bus drive away and instead sat down on the concrete to be with the dying man.

I pulled a chair to the table for her and didn't think of the dishes she had been doing any more than she did.

Twenty minutes passed before she spoke a word to me. "I didn't know there were people who were poor like us." Her emotions were perfectly displayed on her face through her changing expressions: confusion, pity, compassion.

"There are other countries that are poor like Mozambique?" she asked.

I could only nod.

"I didn't know," she said, her tone rising on the last syllable, as if she were asking a question. "I didn't know," she repeated.

I wanted to comfort her. I wanted to shield her from the truth that sometimes felt like it was punching me in the stomach: much of the world was barely surviving.

Zamira was enchanted by the woman in the blue dress.

"What's her name?" she asked. She'd never heard of Mother Teresa.

"Like Mama Aida," she said.

After three or four months Zamira began to trust us. She confided in me that she didn't want to get remarried, because she didn't need the headache. She didn't want someone taking her money, hitting her, or yelling at her children. I could tell she was curious about my husband, because he appeared to be so different from the men she knew. Steve went out of his way to build relationship with her, and he especially enjoyed making her laugh.

One day, he showed her a remote control helicopter that he brought to Mozambique for the kids. When she first saw it, she screamed and ran out of the house, laughing. She stood outside on the porch, at once both timid and curious. Steve handed the remote to her, encouraging her that she could operate it, and like a small girl she giggled with delight as she watched the helicopter ascend into the sky. As was common for those who grew up in the village, she had never had the opportunity to play with toys.

Zamira also was constantly entertained by Steve's disorganization, which he played up for her entertainment. Steve always forgot something, and she found it hilarious when he came back into the house two or three times after leaving for his job on the Iris base. Sometimes she doubled over, her muscular frame plastered against the wall or across the table, laughing so hard she was unable to hold herself up.

A few times a week she imitated Steve's brisk walk and his rushed good morning greeting to her.

"*Bom dia. Bom dia.* (Good morning.)" She said it as quickly as she could get her lips around the words, running the two words into one, trying to keep a straight face as she rushed away, walking in a manner that slightly resembled a chicken. It was her best imitation of Steve, and it always made her cackle. Mozambicans find it especially odd to see people rushing.

Steve received her jests in good humor and attempted to make her laugh even harder. When she asked him a question (in Portuguese), he often replied (in Portuguese), "*Nao falo Portugues. So Makua.* (I don't speak Portuguese. Only Makua.)" This sent her into childlike fits of giggles.

––––––––––––––

It was the middle of the night. Zamira awoke when she heard the shouting. There were two men, or was it three? She couldn't tell, but they were outside of her house. She heard the clatter of what sounded like her washing buckets. A man was cursing.

Her heart began to pound and her throat constricted with fear when her children began to cry. The men were inside the house.

"Where's the money," one of the men shouted. "Where's the money? Give us the money."

They entered her children's room first. It was nearest to the entrance, the place where a wooden door should have been.

"Where's the money?"

They grabbed the children to intimidate them. One of the men struck the frightened kids. Zamira got there just in time to stop another fist from slamming down onto one of her children. They cowered into the beds made from straw rope.

"Mama! Mama!" her children yelled.

"What do you want?" she asked the men through clenched teeth, angry tears falling onto her bare chest. She wore only a cloth wrapped like a nightgown around herself.

"Where's the money?" they repeated. It seemed they knew she had just been paid.

They were soon in Zamira's room searching through her things. One man threw her on the bed and began hitting her— one blow across the face, one across the chest. Blow after blow after blow followed until she couldn't catch her breath. She screamed in pain and fear, asking them to just please take the money and leave.

They continued to beat her.

She had heard stories of *bandidos* (bandits) burning their victims with acid or slashing them with machetes. She was sure they were trying to kill her.

The men kept hitting her. Soon she lost consciousness.

———————

I was recovering from malaria. It was a long, uncomfortable night, my toes getting stuck in the mosquito net and the mosquitoes buzzing just above my head, making me wonder if they were inside or outside of the net. At 3:00 a.m. the rooster was crowing from a nearby tin roof, and there was some scurrying in the other room—rats probably. I tried to ignore the noises, and when I awoke at 8:00 a.m. the sun was high and bright in the sky. I was grateful that Saturday was my day off. My body ached and my head was heavy with fever, but it was hot under the mosquito net and I dragged myself to the couch to wake up slowly.

The air felt sticky with humidity, so I opened the front door, allowing the light in and the warm air to circulate. From the couch I admired the pink and purple bougainvillea flowers we had recently planted in the old canoe we dragged home when it washed up onto the shore.

When I heard a faint tapping on the door to the outside gate, I sank back into the cushions, hoping whoever it was would go away. The door opened slowly, and with great lassitude a woman entered the courtyard.

At first I didn't think I knew her. It was only as she got closer that I noticed her swollen head and the deep purple bruises on her face. Zamira's cheekbone was certainly broken, and her face was so severely damaged that she was hardly the same beautiful woman I had just seen the previous day. The blood had crusted over the wounds.

"Oh, Zamira! What happened?" I asked.

"They robbed me."

"Who robbed you?"

"I don't know. It was the middle of the night. I couldn't see them."

"Zamira…I'm so sorry."

She began to weep. The trauma had made it difficult to cry, but now she wailed as if one of her children had died. She covered her face in her hands, ashamed to be weeping openly. I did the only thing I knew to do and pulled her close to me. Her shoulders were shaking, and tears and snot covered her face as she buried her head into my shoulder. She smelled of sweat and dirt and bodily fluids that hadn't been washed away. She hadn't washed since it happened. She woke up to her kids standing over her, pleading with her to wake up as they shook her unconscious body. Her neighbors helped her get to the hospital. From the hospital she walked to my house.

Because she could hardly stand, we sat on the marble floor of my living room.

Though I felt inadequate, I did my best to comfort her. I willed peace through my arms, pretending to be strong for her, telling her that she was safe now. I could only hope the tears would be some kind of catharsis for her.

This was a woman who was usually ebullient. I cried with her.

After washing and bandaging her wounds and giving her medication for the pain and swelling, my husband and I drove Zamira home to her hut in the hills of the village. We put her in the front seat with pillows to cushion her from the jarring ascent over rocks and dirt humps.

When we neared her house, the sun was still high in the sky, so we parked the car in the dirt lane under one of the only trees, and we walked the narrow and sloping lanes between huts in order to get to hers. There was an eerie silence in her courtyard, and her children were sleeping outside in the shade of the mango tree. Her house was absolutely empty except for the beds made from rope.

The thieves had taken everything: all of her money, the buckets for washing, the few pots, the charcoal, the mosquito nets, blankets, and all of their clothes.

We stayed with her for a while, and when we got up to leave, her forehead creased with fear. We promised that Steve would return later in the afternoon with a door and a lock for her house so that this would not happen again. While he went into the village to purchase what he needed, I went home to gather some clothes and food. I packed three bags: one for her, one for her children, and one with food from our refrigerator and cupboards. We gave her some money to buy the things she'd lost, but we couldn't make her feel safe.

She didn't sleep for months afterward, waiting through the long night, trying not to hold her breath, always willing herself to sleep, hoping the first rays of the sun would shine earlier while trying not to see the men who visited her every night as ghosts.

———————

A few months later I was working on my computer and Zamira was again at our house doing some cleaning. Her wounds had taken a month to heal, and her cheerful tone in the last few weeks told me she was also recovering emotionally.

"*Mana* (Sister), can I ask you something?" Zamira's tone was hesitant.

"Sure," I said, looking up from my work. She leaned the straw broom against the wall and gazed at me intently.

"My daughter, Katarina, just started her monthly cycle. I was wondering if you would talk to her about it. Can you explain to her what it means to be a woman?"

"What do you mean?" I said.

"Well, she got it last month too, and the tradition is to celebrate her womanhood by inviting all of our neighbors to eat
a feast at our house. I don't want to do this, though. They don't
care about her. They just want to eat, and I don't have money
for that nonsense." Zamira spoke candidly, telling me what
she really thought rather than what she thought I wanted to
hear, as she had done at first in our relationship.

"Have you explained what this means to Katarina yet?" I
asked.

"I told her how to wear rags so it doesn't come through her
skirt, but I don't know what to tell her about being a woman.
I was hoping we could celebrate her womanhood by coming
here for a little party where you and a few others could explain
what being a woman means."

I didn't even have children yet. My own cultural bias was
that it was a mother's role to talk to her daughter about being
a woman. I encouraged Zamira to talk to her daughter openly.

"But I don't know what to say," she responded.

Zamira was at a loss, and so was I. I was uncomfortable,
much like I was when a woman from the village asked me
to breast-feed her sixteen-month-old son. When I explained
that I didn't have any milk, she didn't mind at all, because she
didn't either. Evidently nipples were the communal pacifiers.

"You're my daughter and mother," Zamira said. I wasn't
entirely sure what she meant, but I didn't want to ruin the
sweetness of the moment by asking for clarification. On an
intuitive level I understood.

———————————

"You're so beautiful!" Zamira said to me one morning as I
walked out of my bedroom wearing a long flowing skirt.

She had come to wash our laundry and wanted to get started before it was too unbearably hot outside; the sun was relentless after 9:30 in the morning. She stopped sorting the clothes when I came out.

"Everyone says you're the prettiest woman. My friends always talk about you when you walk by. They say, 'she is the most beautiful one,' and they imitate the graceful way you walk. Others walk like this," she said. She strode purposefully forward, swinging her arms and walking fast with a masculine gait, imitating the gait of other women. "No," she said, shaking her head in disapproval and wagging her finger. Zamira and I doubled over in hysterics, enjoying her theatrics and the intimacy of the secret joke. Later she braided my hair.

Zamira was gorgeous too, in her fitted cotton shirt, brightly colored wrap skirt, and matching head wrap, the bright colors symbolic and defiant in the face of the kind of darkness she had faced and overcome. Uncannily her name means nightingale, which reminded me of the woman in the Greek myth who was raped and silenced and then transformed into a nightingale. As one writer observed, the woman in this myth was able to "subvert the patriarchy that would subjugate her by usurping the power of language into a call to sisterhood."[2]

In Mozambique Zamira taught me that the human spirit could sing, like the nightingale, even in the dark.

After three years in Mozambique, Steve and I were leaving for an extended time away. We'd be gone for at least six months, and we wanted to give Zamira a gift.

As a surprise we arranged to fix her house—adding a tin roof to stop the rain and a bamboo fence for security and privacy. Only a few months earlier she had asked us to hold on to some of the money we were to pay her so she could buy a tin roof once she had saved enough money. She had only a grass roof that leaked cold water into the mud rooms when the rains came. We marveled that she would to choose to live on less, which meant very little food for her and her family, in order to save for the future.

I hoped the excitement about her remodeled house would make it easier for her to hear that we would be gone for a while. She was cleaning the bedroom when I asked if I could talk with her.

We sat at the kitchen table together as I explained that we'd be leaving. Her dark brown eyes narrowed into slits.

"For how long?"

"Four to six months." I explained we had work to do for an organization in Europe. I didn't tell her that we would also enjoy a break from the hardships of daily life in Pemba. The constant crises took a toll on most everyone.

Before I finished speaking, she rushed out of the room. When I went into the bedroom where she had gone, I found her sitting on the edge of the bed against the mosquito net, sobbing. She covered her face with her hands, her long slender fingers pressed tightly against her eyes.

"Zamira...I'm so sorry."

Explaining that we would call her from Europe, that we would certainly return, and even that we found replacement work for her with the person who would house-sit for us didn't help at all.

When I introduced her to the girl who would house-sit for us, Zamira was timid and acted shy. Later Zamira complained that she didn't know her. She worried aloud that the girl would treat her poorly.

Four weeks after we left, I dreamed I was back in Mozambique. My dreams often took place in Africa, but when I awoke from this one, I wanted to speak to Zamira. It was 6:00

a.m. where we were in Europe and 7:00 a.m. in Mozambique. Because Zamira didn't have a phone, my husband and I called the girl who was staying in our house. Zamira had arrived already at the house and was sweeping the patio and watering the plants, which had blossomed wildly under her care.

We were as excited as children as we dialed the number; Zamira would be surprised to hear from us. We didn't know if she had ever used a phone.

"Hello?"

"Zamira?"

"*Mana?* (Sister?) *Mano* Steve? (Brother Steve?)"

"Zamira! How are you?"

"*Mana*, Oh, *Mana*..." There was a lovely soft "h" on the last syllables and a singsong voice of wistfulness and longing.

"*Temos saudades de voce!* (We miss you!)"

"*Mana! Mana! Mano!*" Zamira began to literally scream with joy.

Then she started laughing hysterically. We chuckled at the sounds of her unbridled happiness.

"How are you?" I asked.

"*Mana!*"

We got no response to our questions. Every time we spoke, she laughed harder. Zamira's laughter rang in our ears, until we couldn't even hear our own questions. It was so contagious that finally we couldn't contain our laughter, which mingled with hers, the minutes passing as quickly as dreams in the night while tears of joy streamed down my face. We couldn't stop laughing.

Most of the conversation was not really words at all.

———————————

Zamira's story was not uncommon. One of the harder adjustments for me in Mozambique was seeing the status of women in Mozambican society. Their status could be seen by the way they always walked behind the men on the dusty street or in the crowded market stalls. The women stood out because of their beautifully colored traditional clothes while the men wore standard Western T-shirts and pants.

The men in the villages had multiple wives, if you could even call it marriage. Most Mozambican men didn't have enough money for a wedding or to pay a *lobolo* (bride price), so when a man saw a woman he liked, he just walked into her bedroom. He might stay a few weeks or months or maybe even years, but usually after a short time he grew bored and went to cohabit with someone else, leaving behind a woman who would be desperate to find another man. Most women had no way to provide for themselves or their children without a man. Sometimes a woman's brothers might help her. Because Zamira had found a job, she was an exception, but the mere fact that she was a woman made her vulnerable.

Iris's mercy ministry was an outreach to widows and vulnerable women such as Zamira in the Pemba community. Instead of just giving handouts to the widows and disabled men, the program had developed in such a way that they were organized into smaller groups who made crafts for the ministry to sell.

Of all the tasks involved with running the mercy ministry, the food distribution was especially hard. Some of the widows were mean. It took time, but I came to understand that they were mean because they were fighting for survival. They became the most anxious or angry over food. In the beginning of the program the Mozambican female leader measured out the food in front of the two hundred women in line, which was a very bad idea because it enabled them to argue over just how much they were given. "That woman received more" and "this is not enough" were the most common complaints.

They stood in the hot sun for up to four hours waiting for their five kilos of beans and eight kilos of rice. They shouted and pushed and jeered. One of the widows got so angry she slapped me on the arm. I was merely watching the distribution process and had no idea why she was angry. The team eventually realized they were able to alleviate some of the tension by measuring the food beforehand, but measuring out the rice and dry beans in a hot warehouse was still tedious work.

The lowest point of the ministry was when one of the Mozambican leaders involved in the program, a man in his twenties, was arrested for abusing the child of one of the widows. The girl was eight years old.

The day it happened, she had asked her mother if she could play on the playground with the other kids. The man went to the playground and found her, telling her he would give her a necklace and twenty mets (less than a dollar) if she went with him into the storage closet.

The widows were furious. The man went to jail.

Then, a week later, he was out of prison and standing in front of me putting his hand out for me to shake. I looked at him wondering what to do. In those ten seconds while I pondered whether or not to shake his hand, I remembered something Heidi had once told me.

In a moment in her life similar to the one I was encountering, Heidi had had to make the same decision to choose between forgiveness for a man who had hurt someone she loved or allowing bitterness to stay in the pit of her stomach till the end of her days. She found forgiveness so difficult that the only thing she could think to do was ask the offender to pray for her because she needed more love. She knelt down in front of him. The offender placed his hand on her head and asked God to bless her.

So I shook his hand, bestowing on him not acceptance of

his crime but acceptance of his humanity, both the dignity and the shame. It did not excuse what he had done, and I really wasn't sure what I thought about the mother's decision to tell the police not to keep him in jail because she didn't want to see him sentenced to sixteen years in prison. Despite the woman's leniency, he was losing his job at the children's center. The other children needed to be protected from him.

He argued to try to keep his job, but only weakly, and he wanted to know if he could still attend the Iris church he was part of in Pemba. The pastor recommended that he go to a much smaller Iris church closer to his home—one that didn't have hundreds of children running around.

When the man left, we prayed for the mother of the girl and told her that we were so sorry. We were as appalled as she was. We made sure she knew that the man would not be permitted to work at Iris anymore. The only emotion she showed was when she emitted a guttural noise of disgust as she told us again about his offer to give her eight-year-old daughter twenty mets for sex.

———————

Pastor Tanueque, a national pastor from the Nampula province of Mozambique, visited Pemba for two months to teach in the Mozambican Bible school. It was the first time he had ever been away from his wife. In a cultural workshop for the international missions school students, he explained the relationship between men and women in Mozambique as he saw it.

He started off by explaining a cultural norm: Mozambican men often beat their wives. For instance, if the man could not find one of his socks, he would chase his wife around the house. As an aside he said, "There are some naughty women who beat their husbands." Mostly though, he acknowledged, the men were in charge. According to him the men got all of the credit. When someone was healed from a physical infirmity, the people would say, "The pastor healed him or her," even if it was the wife who did the actual praying.

"But I have learned from my wife," Pastor Tanueque said.

Once, when a small girl from their village died, the child's family brought her body to the Tanueques' house, where it would remain until the next day when the morgue opened. No one was expecting a miracle.

Mrs. Tanueque went into the living room where the girl's body was, and she prayed diligently, unrelentingly. After two hours the child opened her eyes.

After telling this story, Pastor Tanueque said, "My wife also has authority in the house. I'm grateful for how she showed strength in the past." Then, humbly, he continued, "When I was a big drunk, my wife was the one who took me to church and believed for me."

Pastor Tanueque continued further: "When your wife is angry, don't make her angrier. When there's an argument, someone has to be quiet, and that person is me. A woman needs to be treated with care, affection. Go to the market and buy her a *capulana* or some fish. She'll be happy with fish."

When Mrs. Tanueque was in the Iris Bible school, she couldn't pass any of her exams because she didn't know how to read or write. The director of the Bible school mentioned to Heidi that Mrs. Tanueque would not be able to graduate because of this.

Heidi exclaimed, "She raised a baby from the dead in Jesus's name! She is graduating!"

Mrs. Tanueque spent much of her time in the local provinces teaching other women. Her faith was an example to them all, and many asked her specifically about the times she prayed for people who had died and then came back to life as a result of her prayers.

Pastor Tanueque concluded his talk with this: "I married my wife March 3, 1972, and we started living together at 10:00 p.m., and we've been together until now. I didn't know what marriage was when we got married. I just went to sleep. After a month I finally discovered what marriage was."

At this comment everyone laughed and cheered and clapped, but I'm sure they also appreciated the way he advocated for women's rights. It was a good reminder that culture was not homogenous, and stereotyping was never helpful. In every culture there were diverse groups. And there were always ones like Pastor Tanueque, who would fight for change, who would be a voice for those who were not heard.

On a day in late March a man from Kentucky arrived on the Pemba base. The man, dressed in casual business clothes, dress shoes, and a wide-brimmed hat, was from the Gideon association. He wanted to meet Heidi Baker. A pastor friend had asked him if he knew of her, and when he said he didn't, the pastor recommended he stop by to meet her.

The man showed up at Heidi's office, and one of her personal assistants asked if he was willing just to talk to someone else who represented the ministry.

"Do you have to talk to Heidi directly?" she asked. Everyone always wanted to talk to Heidi directly, but Heidi was already in a meeting and would be in meetings all day. The man didn't relent; he wanted to speak to Heidi.

"Can you come back tomorrow at 2:30?" She could fit him in for ten minutes. He did return the next day, and while he was waiting to see Heidi, he left six hundred Portuguese New Testaments for the ministry to distribute.

Instead of ten minutes his meeting with Heidi lasted more than two hours, and he agreed to donate thirty thousand more New Testaments. One of the requirements, however, was that they must be distributed through men; women could not be Gideons.

"OK," Heidi said good-naturedly, "We have men. Here are the men." She introduced him to the men in the ministry and encouraged the men in Iris leadership to sign up as Gideons. No big deal; they could be Gideons too. Why not?

She smiled inwardly, completely secure in herself, a female leader of a massive movement who had just received thirty thousand free Bibles. To the Mozambican women Heidi was a forerunner, a leader whom men followed.

Part V

COMING BACK

Chapter 19

SAY GOOD-BYE

I**T WAS EARLY** 2009 and Iris was growing in extraordinary ways. Although Heidi and Rolland's lives were being multiplied through their adopted and spiritual children, and expansion was taking place all around them, Rolland was still in the throes of dementia. It had started a year or two earlier when he came down with cerebral malaria. His ability to think clearly was severely limited, and instead of getting better as everyone hoped, Rolland's health was still declining in every way.

Alberto was one of those adopted into the Iris family, and he held a special place in Heidi and Rolland's heart. Alberto, a man in his late twenties, was fluent in Portuguese and English, and sometimes served as a translator in the Bible school classes. He moved from Maputo to Pemba a few years earlier to help Heidi and Rolland. Alberto assisted Heidi with her own projects when she went on outreaches, but his main role these days was caring for Rolland, going to the Bakers' house to check on him at least two or three times a day. When Rolland slept too long, Alberto woke him, asking him to please get up and eat the food he had prepared for him. When Rolland was grouchy or sarcastic or just completely unresponsive, Alberto merely laughed good-naturedly and continued gently talking to Rolland, the man who was like a father to him.

Alberto didn't know what happened to his biological father. When his father disappeared, abandoning Alberto and his mother, they journeyed to live in the city with his mother's parents. But soon afterward Alberto's mother remarried, and as is often the case in Mozambique, the stepfather didn't like Alberto. It was one thing not to be liked, but it was another thing altogether to watch his stepfather scream and abuse his mother. Alberto was only eight years old when he decided to return to his grandparents' house to live.

Unfortunately even his grandparents viewed this small, scrawny boy as little more than a domestic servant, the typical way Mozambican families viewed children who lived with them who weren't their own. It was common that the children were expected to pay for their board through labor.

Alberto's grandparents woke him up at 4:00 a.m. each day, making him fetch water for the family, which meant carrying a heavy bucket of water on his head. When he said it was too heavy, they ridiculed him for being weak, and then they beat him. He would hide in the kitchen when he was in trouble, sleeping on the floor and hoping they wouldn't see him. When they did find him, they beat him so badly he had scars for years afterward. Sometimes they didn't feed him for three days.

Eventually Alberto realized that living on the street would be better.

He didn't suffer much on the street because he had a charismatic personality that gave him favor with people. A Portuguese woman wanted to take him back to Portugal with her and adopt him as her son; a South African man who owned a butcher shop sometimes fed him meat. Another expatriate woman took him to her house with her on the weekends.

Alberto met Heidi after he had been on the street for three years; he was twelve years old. It took him four long weeks to decide to live at the center with Heidi and Rolland. She visited him while he was sitting on the corner with his street friends. Heidi told Alberto that Jesus loved him. When she prayed for him, she told him she knew he had suffered much but God wanted to heal the hurt in his heart. As he looked out into the street, his eyes moved past the familiar shops, past the bits of garbage strewn along the road, past the straw mat on which he slept at night, on toward the ocean far in the distance, and he could actually feel the anger going away.

He decided to take a chance and go home with her.

Alberto recounted countless funny stories to me of Mama Heidi, calling her by her English name rather than Mama Aida. She loved to play, which made him and all the kids adore her. She often took them to the white sandy beach in Bilene, even though it was a three-hour drive. Alberto had so much fun because she drove more than 85 miles an hour, and they shouted and laughed and talked the whole way there. Alberto recounted how Mama Heidi always knew if something was wrong, and she was always there to listen, pray, and comfort them.

Alberto told me little about Papa Rolland in the early years, but it was obvious by the way he cared for him with such gentle patience and dignity while Rolland was suffering from dementia that he had great love and respect for him.

It was evident that Rolland's sickness and everything else Heidi carried on her shoulders was really weighing on her, and one morning in Pemba she asked a few of us to come to the small private prayer room to pray for her personally. One other missionary was there, as well as one of Heidi's good friends, who was a Catholic nun from the south of France.

Though the door was closed, the village kids ran up to it and turned the knob, pushing the door open and running away. It was certainly keeping them entertained, their laughs echoing across the garden filled with bright pink and purple bougainvillea blossoms, but after the third time the door flew open, Heidi asked us to turn the key in the lock. She hardly ever shut the kids out of anything, often personally inviting them into the most important meetings.

When we finally settled down onto the concrete floor, Heidi lay down on her back on a mat in the middle of the room. It was a sign she was exhausted, but it was also a posture of surrender and open-handedness toward God. "This is hard for me," she said. She spoke in a terse tone, which I had rarely heard from her before.

"A few months ago the doctors tested Rolland with thirty questions, and he scored a twenty-five out of thirty, which meant he had slight dementia. They said it was progressive. They warned me it could happen quickly..." Her voice trailed off and she paused, taking a deep breath and looking up at the ceiling. The Catholic sister took Heidi's hand and held onto it. The similarities between the two women struck me as unique. One was single and the other one was married, but they both had dedicated their lives to the same single purpose of loving Jesus and others.

"Lately I noticed he's been more confused and when I asked him to speak to the villagers, he paused for long periods of time and didn't know what to say. I haven't seen him like this before." She paused again, then she continued hesitantly. "I asked the doctor to test him again." Her voice trailed off, seemingly lost in her own thoughts. "When the doctor asked him what country he was in, he said America. When Rolland was asked where he was last week, he said Platypus Island. When they asked him what day of the week it was, he got it wrong. He scored a sixteen out of thirty, which means the dementia is severe now."

"Oh, Heidi, I'm so sorry," I said, taking her other hand in mine.

"They told me he might even begin to forget me. They said

I need to get a full-time caregiver for him." Her voice broke, and she began to weep.

The two others started to pray for her then; there was not much to say that could help. We prayed for comfort for Heidi, for Rolland's healing, for help from others, for peace.

Heidi spoke to God out of her sadness and desperation, and she spoke to Him like He was as familiar to her as one of us.

"God, I know You are always good—and that You can turn this around for good. Thank You for the visa Rolland got last year so he can stay in Mozambique, where full-time caregivers are even less expensive than they are in the States. Thank You that there is a family here who will love him and take care of him," Heidi prayed. "God, let us learn through this situation— even more—that people are valuable just for who they are, not for what they can do. I don't want to be driven, and I don't want to drive anyone. Let us know more of the rhythm of Your heartbeat, Your rest, and how to love one another."

She paused in her prayer, her eyelids fluttering slightly. "Please give us the resources we need to feed the hungry children here in Mozambique's provinces," she continued. "You know what we need. Thank you for this family here; in the end it's all we're left with."

Finances were weighing heavily on Heidi too. It was 2009, and the financial crisis in the United States had heavily affected donations, which were down by half. Heidi was aware that people were losing houses, jobs, and cars. She didn't blame them for not being able to give, but it didn't change the fact that she had to meet a hefty monthly budget so the children would be fed, clothed, and educated; the workers' salaries would be paid; and the buildings would be completed. Heidi wasn't sure where the money they needed was going to come from. Now that Rolland wasn't able to write newsletters and update people about their work, many of the Iris staff wondered if people who had supported them in the past might forget about them.

Donations usually came in from all over the world. They came from people who wanted to give to the general budget, sometimes twenty or forty dollars at a time. Occasionally individual donors gave large donations, but it was definitely the exception rather than the rule. Donations also came from churches that wanted to support Heidi and Rolland's work in Mozambique or that wanted to give to specific projects like drilling a clean water well for a bush village, which cost about six thousand dollars. Usually when Heidi spoke at churches or conferences, it reminded people about their work, so the people in Iris's finance office believed that having enough money was always partially contingent on Heidi and Rolland traveling and speaking.

They didn't do it for this reason, though. They traveled because they genuinely wanted to bless people in the West too, especially after what Heidi learned through her experiences with the blind women named Aida. Before he was sick, Rolland often addressed finances head-on in his presentations, as he tended to enjoy being controversial. He would say something like: "We could go around looking morose and telling you a bunch of sad stories in order to guilt you into giving, but that wouldn't be fun for anyone, and God wouldn't get any of the glory. Instead we tell you about all the amazing things God is doing among us so you will be blessed and encouraged in your faith."

They believed there were two sides to things, and they saw the neediness on both sides of the equation. The poor were needy physically and materially, but the Western world was impoverished emotionally and spiritually. Depression was unprecedented in those places while the real and genuine community the third world knew how to cultivate was the perfect antidote to depression. Material resources were not the only indicator of well-being.

Heidi encouraged missionaries to see the hidden poverty in the West instead of judging them for being blind to the developing world. Sometimes people in the West were deeply unhappy, but this poverty was on the inside; it was not visible and thus harder to see.

Networks of individuals in the United Kingdom and Canada had sprung up in their respective countries to receive private donations for Iris's work among the poor. They merely collected it and sent it to Mozambique, where it went into the work on the ground, virtually none of it being spent for administrative costs, which was unique for this type of organization. Iris was mostly fueled by missionaries, who were volunteers. The Mozambican staff were paid salaries, but this helped boost the economy and gave the people a fair wage for their work.

She couldn't imagine having to leave her home in Mozambique to go back to the United States because of Rolland's sickness. She knew people might not understand, but in many ways she felt it was better and easier in Mozambique for both of them.

After the prayer time Heidi told the missionary who helped her with daily details like grocery shopping that she would not need any food this week. She had actually gotten up extra early this morning to prepare a tuna casserole so they'd have something to eat without having to spend money on groceries.

She was serious, the situation appearing so bleak to her that no one dared try to persuade her that there *was* money enough to buy food for them.

Heidi was about to embark on another world speaking tour, where she would be gone from Mozambique for just over a month. "I don't want to go," she complained. Heidi knew

Alberto would take good care of Rolland, but with all the other pressing issues Heidi felt overwhelmed. She didn't even know which countries she was going to until her assistant handed her the itinerary.

When Heidi returned four weeks later, Rolland met her at the airport. He waited for her in the restaurant on the second floor where he could watch the plane land. As soon as he saw the plane approaching, while it was still in the sky, he leaped up from the small table and almost ran down the steps, even though it would take another fifteen minutes for Heidi to pass through customs.

Rolland paced anxiously as he waited. When he couldn't wait any longer, he walked up to the door where she would exit and stood just outside of it, looking in through the glass like a child waiting impatiently. Though it was rare for him to show emotion these days, Rolland seemed so excited to see Heidi. When she finally stepped out, he embraced her.

Then, as usual, he waited in the background for her while her children and coworkers welcomed her home, everyone vying for her attention all at once. Rolland walked to the car without her. Then he walked back to her. He walked halfway to the car again, and then came back. This was hard for them both.

For almost two years Heidi had been caring for him while he struggled to remember who and where he was and slept away most every day.

Over the next few weeks the doctor continued to touch base with them by phone and to give Rolland cognitive tests.

His decline was steady, and when Rolland was almost completely gone mentally and physically, the doctor advised Heidi that it was time to say good-bye. Soon he would stop swallowing.

She should notify the family.

Heidi contacted their biological children, Elisha and Crystalyn, who were living in the United States, and booked their flights to Pemba.

It tore at her heart to tell her children: "Please come say good-bye to Dad."

Chapter 20

IN NEED OF A MIRACLE

F OR ALL THE supernatural experiences they'd had in their travels through Asia, England, and Africa, Heidi and Rolland were never focused on the miracles. Their focus was always on the people—on loving them. Miracles happened, but they were just part of the whole. This was true in every sense, but Heidi still had trouble understanding why God was healing others and not Rolland. Every week she went into the bush of Mozambique, and the deaf heard; it was so easy. Even when others on her team, both foreigners and nationals, prayed for the deaf, still they were healed. Heidi simply didn't understand.

On a typical Thursday afternoon in Pemba, the work of the day was winding down as the African sun dipped a little lower in the sky, and a team of fifty people (missionaries, Mozambicans, visitors, and kids) prepared for the weekly bush outreach.

Steve and I had been living in Pemba full time for four years, long enough for it to feel like home, but our friends Tim and Anna were visiting us for the first time, getting their very first taste of Africa, their first experience in a developing country. Anna joked that she hardly ever even left her tristate area, and Tim made a sarcastic remark about their privileged lives. They were all smiles, excited for the adventure into the bush.

Some of the team tied the tents, sleeping bags, and typical camping gear to the top of our vehicles, and when the supplies, food, and water were loaded, we searched for the visitors who had wandered from the group because they were tired and bored of waiting. The Western visitors were the only ones who were keeping track of the time and who cared that we were leaving more than an hour later than planned.

As we drove out of the front gate of Ministerio Arco-Iris, as it's known in Portuguese, the sunlight was departing, shades of tangerine streaking the sky above the giant baobab trees. At that time of day the Indian Ocean across from the base looked pink, the smell of saltwater drifted through the air, and the hectic pace of the day slowed as the heat was whisked away by the departing sun.

The bush, way out in the interior of Mozambique where there's hardly any connection to the outside world, seemed to be isolated, but for the people who called it home, their tiny community was just that—a community. It was all they had ever known with no exposure to anything else, no way to know they were cut off from the larger world.

Anna and Tim were noticing the basics of sub-Saharan Africa: the mud houses served only as shade from the sun and substandard protection from deadly mosquitoes at night. The people lived, cooked, and ate outside. The deep-red African soil, the shining green foliage, and the bright sunshine were trademarks of day in the bush—the deep, milky darkness and the brilliant stars blanketing the sky were the trademarks of night. There was no electricity for hundreds of miles.

The village to which we were headed was a three-and-a-half-hour drive away, an hour of which was on the paved road, the other two-and-a-half hours over dirt roads and potholes so deep you had to be careful not to hit your head on the roof of the vehicle. There were ten of us crowded into the back cab of the Land Rover, squeezing together on benches that typically held six.

Tim asked questions about the country and culture while

Anna remained quiet, until suddenly, unrelated to the conversation, she exclaimed, "What am I doing?" Her voice was a little louder than normal with undertones of panic in it.

"What have we gotten ourselves into? We are out here in the middle of nowhere!" She laughed nervously, trying to make light of her rising feelings of panic.

When we arrived in the village, it was so dark it was hard to tell it was even a village. It seemed we stopped in the middle of the dirt road. The field we were in was actually not any different from the road; it had the same hard-packed dirt with no grass or ground cover. We could barely see the few mud huts at the edge of the field. It was as if we'd gone back in time, where there was no electricity or running water, only a hole in the ground to use for a toilet.

The first thing we did was set up our tents in the yard outside one of the mud huts so we would be protected by the goodwill of the person who was letting us stay in his or her yard. We needed someone to vouch for us, to say that we were there because they wanted us to be. Often we had valuable things like cameras and iPods stolen when someone from the village cut through the side of the tent with a machete and removed the items inside. If someone respected in the community vouched for us, this was much less likely to happen because we would be viewed more as guests than as outsiders with an agenda.

Tim and Anna set their tent up directly across from ours, and then we left our camping area to join the crowd in the field, where *The Jesus Film* was being shown in the Makua language. It may have been the first time the villagers had ever seen a film. We brought our own generators to power the film, which was projected onto a huge white screen. The generator also powered one light that shone down onto the crowd. This was not a huge crusade—just an unannounced informal gathering around our flatbed truck, which held the sound system and the screen.

One Makua man asked, "Where is Jesus right now?"

Another villager responded, "He is in Jerusalem." This was the name of the city he had heard the disciples say in the film.

"When is He coming here?" The images in the film mirrored the images the Mozambicans saw in their everyday lives. The film showed men fishing and people eating loaves of bread and fish with the heads still on them. In the film they traveled by foot on dirt roads—like the Mozambicans traveled.

Some of the villagers thought they were watching news footage of Jesus, and they hoped Jesus would soon arrive in Mozambique to perform the same miracles they saw Him doing in the film.

When the film ended, someone from our team spoke to the people. He told them there was a God who loved them and that Jesus came to earth to show them who God was and to save them from death and disease. To illustrate our message, Heidi asked if there were any people in the village who were deaf. She had done this many times. More often than not, there was at least one person in the village who could not hear.

Anna and Tim were interested observers; they stood a little off to the right in the front of the crowd of people. Steve and I translated for them, interpreting the language and the events.

There was a small commotion in the back on the right side of the crowd, and people were pushing a man to the front. Heidi asked if he was deaf; they nodded and shouted that he was. Heidi put her fingers on his ears and prayed for less than a minute, and suddenly he was smiling. There were no lightning bolts or thunder, nothing to announce this miracle but a man's smile.

He was smiling because he could hear. Heidi spoke to him

in his language, saying *"Alelu Jesu.* (Thank You, Jesus.)" He repeated it after her four, five, six times.

"Alelu Jesu."

Just then, a tall, skinny man from the back yelled to the front that he was going to get his son and to wait for him to return.

The crowd was abuzz with excitement. Then a man who appeared intoxicated stumbled forward and reached for the translator's microphone. "You say that this man, my friend, can now hear. But how do I know that he can hear?"

Before anyone could answer, the healed man grabbed the microphone and spoke loudly into it, saying, "But I hear what you have just asked. You can know that I'm healed because I've just heard you and am now telling you myself that I can hear you." In the back of the crowd, some of the elders laughed loudly at this reply, mocking the drunk man who asked the question in the first place.

The crowd was talking amongst themselves, and before Tim and Anna could even begin to comprehend the magnitude of what had happened, a small boy was pushed forward to Heidi.

The boy appeared to be eight or nine years old, which meant he may have been ten or eleven. Slightly bewildered, he was not sure why he was taken out of his bed to stand at the front of this crowd.

Heidi welcomed the boy and waved him to come closer. She smiled at him. Then she embraced him. She held him for a few minutes before she asked him if he could hear. He smiled shyly and raised his eyebrows, which was the equivalent of nodding one's head yes. She took his hand and put it on her vocal cords and let him feel the vibration as she said, *"Aleleu Jesu."*

Then she put his hand on his own vocal cords, asking him to try.

His first words were, "*Alelu Jesu.*" Unlike the other man, he struggled to wrap his tongue around the syllables. It was obvious that he had been born deaf and this was the first time he was speaking.

The tall, skinny man who ran to get his son was exclamatory in his statements: "He can hear! He can go to school now! He can hear!" He was jumping up and down. It was the most expressive response I had seen from a Mozambican. "I used to send him to school, but he couldn't understand anything. He stopped going, but now he can go back to school!" This meant everything for the boy and his family. An education was the only hope for a better life.

I translated to Tim and Anna. The man's joy was contagious, and we were all rejoicing together and laughing as he continued to talk animatedly.

"Isn't this amazing?" I asked Tim and Anna, still moved every time I saw something like it.

Tim was grappling to understand what had just happened. He asked again for clarity: "So the boy can hear now?"

I reiterated what the boy's father was saying and why he was rejoicing so loudly.

"Isn't it amazing?" I repeated mostly to myself, wrapped up in what was going on but trying to be a good host for my friends at the same time.

"No," Anna said. There was a look of pure bewilderment on her face.

"What do you mean?" I asked, still watching the scene unfolding before us.

"I don't think it's amazing at all."

"Why? Two people were deaf, and now they can hear."

But Anna was looking in the other direction. Hardly aware

of what was going on at the front of the crowd with the boy
or his father, Anna was looking at the hundreds of people
standing in the dirt, the dust particles in the air shining like
crystals in the only light.

"I think it's awful."

"What's wrong? What's awful?" I didn't understand.

"Look at all these people."

I looked at the crowd of people and tried to remember what
I saw the first time I came to the bush.

Then I understood. What she was seeing was the poor, and
she was seeing them, *really* seeing them, for the first time in
her life.

Men and women were huddled together, many of them
barefoot because they didn't own shoes. The women wore
pieces of cloth tied around their waists to make a long skirt,
but their shirts were discolored and stretched thin, and many
of the men wore T-shirts with holes in them. The whites of
their eyes were yellow, and their teeth were blackened by the
sugar cane they ate trying to dull the hunger pains in their
stomachs.

The children were covered in a layer of dirt; many of the
babies were naked, peeing on whoever held them. Anna was
also probably smelling the odor of unwashed bodies. With no
supply of water in this village, the people walked for miles
to fetch the water they needed. After cooking and drinking,
there was little left for bathing.

Tears were filling Anna's eyes. I realized then what was happening for her, and I stopped interpreting for her, allowing her
to absorb what she was experiencing.

Soon the crowd was dispersing, and we headed to our tents
for the evening. The Mozambican team who came with us
cooked dinner for everyone over the fire—plain spaghetti

with tuna fish, and they passed around plastic plates filled to the brim with long, sticky noodles and canned tuna.

After dinner we said good night but saw one another again as we walked a few yards away from the tents to brush our teeth with water from our water bottles spilling out onto the dry ground. It was hard not to wonder what the villagers thought of us with our equipment, tents, and material possessions. What we brought with us for one night just about equaled all of their worldly possessions.

As Steve and I drifted off to sleep, listening to the voices of our team members around us, we heard Anna's faint cries and Tim trying to comfort her. The first experience of such poverty had rocked her, telling us that more than just two lives were transformed that night.

A professor of religious studies from Indiana University traveled to Pemba, Mozambique, to conduct a research study. Dr. Candy Brown wanted to quantitatively measure the results of Heidi and her team's prayers on Mozambicans who were deaf and/or blind. The results of the study were astounding, proving that the miracles and healings were not fabricated or merely the power of suggestion. To Heidi and her team the findings were merely another piece of good news because the quantifiable research proved only what they already knew.

Brown's "Study of the Therapeutic Effects of Proximal Intercessory Prayer (STEPP) on Auditory and Visual Impairments in Rural Mozambique" was published in the September 2010 issue of the *Southern Medical Journal*. The study used an audiometer to test the individual Mozambicans' hearing levels, and for those who had vision problems, the clinical researchers used vision charts. The results surely baffled some of the researchers, who made sure they checked with precision, according to the study's guidelines. After receiving prayer, the Mozambicans could hear and see.

For the skeptics who might claim that it was merely the power of suggestion or hypnosis, Dr. Brown stated that the healing results were far greater and more significant than studies have shown about the miniscule improvements that come from hypnosis and suggestion.

One of her conclusions was that future study should determine whether intercessory prayer "may be a useful adjunct to standard medical care for certain patients with auditory and/or visual impairments, especially in contexts where access to conventional treatment is limited."[1]

———————

Anna's favorite little boy on the Pemba base was Akhil. When she first spotted him, Akhil was wearing a bright yellow T-shirt with a red heart on the front. Anna's personal motto was "Love is the answer," and she loved all things heart shaped. When we took her snorkeling in front of the Pemba base, she even found a heart-shaped fragment of coral reef.

Akhil had been born with a deformity that prevented him from walking easily, but he didn't allow his disability to define him. He taught himself to do everything the other kids did so easily. He ran as fast as they did; he did the same tricks on the playground monkey bars; he performed flips in the sand, and he was a great dancer. He learned how to do the moonwalk as well as how to breakdance and spin on his head and arms.

Akhil was about eight years old, and he was cheeky. He had a grin as wide as the sky, and he usually got whatever he wanted through a combination of his smile, his searching dark-brown eyes, and his plaintive little boy voice. To top it off, he was outgoing and funny! Everyone loved Akhil, especially Mama Aida. She was putty in his hands.

"Mama Aida, Mama Aida, I'm going on outreach with you!" Akhil exclaimed every Thursday afternoon.

Mama Aida's assent was all he needed to override the list the children's center director drew up every week to determine whose turn it was to go on outreach. The children rotated so they would all have a chance to go periodically. But almost every week, without fail, Akhil climbed his way into the back of Mama Aida's vehicle.

In one of the villages there was a four- or five-year-old girl who was unable to walk. Heidi described the little girl's legs as "jelly legs." As soon as Akhil saw the girl, he marched up to her. When Akhil reached the little girl, he put his hands on her shoulders and said confidently, "In the name of Jesus."

Instantly the little girl's legs straightened and were able to support the weight of her body. They watched as the girl's mother held her hands above her head as she took her very first steps.

In that moment Heidi couldn't have been prouder of Akhil.

Many in the village, who were of a different faith background, came to believe in Jesus, who healed the little girl through a little boy not much older than her.

Sometimes it just didn't make sense. Akhil could pray for a little girl with jelly legs and see her healed while he continued to hobble around.

It was like Heidi seeing the deaf healed week after week while Rolland lay on his deathbed.

Chapter 21

GERMANY

AFTER LEARNING FROM an old friend of Rolland's about an alternative treatment clinic in Europe, Heidi agreed to try this new option. Surely it was better than just giving in to the death sentence Rolland had received. All expenses were supposed to be paid, so with their children still in Pemba, Heidi left to escort Rolland to the clinic in Europe.

Heidi stayed with Rolland for a little while at the clinic in Germany before returning to Mozambique. The naturopath doctor advised Heidi that Rolland's adrenals had shut down altogether, and it could take many months to revitalize them. It also appeared that Rolland may have had mini strokes as a result of the cerebral malaria he had contracted previously. The clinic told him that his whole system needed to be rebuilt through careful monitoring and vitamins and nutrients administered intravenously.

In Pemba, a month or so later, we all heard that Rolland was improving slightly and that he was now taking long walks in the German countryside.

We also heard about the extremely high medical bill that continued to grow with every treatment. There was a misunderstanding, and the clinic was not treating Rolland pro bono. Now the Bakers had to come up with thousands of dollars from their personal income for Rolland's care. It was a shock.

Even more surprising was the e-mail Rolland abruptly sent out to friends and family around the world shortly after he left Mozambique. It was titled "Coming Back."[1]

Coming Back
Rolland and Heidi Baker
Iris Ministries
Pemba, Mozambique
21 June 2009

I am surrounded by the rolling green hills of western Germany. Rich groves of shade trees line the winding country lane on which I am taking my daily prayer walk. The day is beautiful, filled with blue sky and brilliant clouds. Cows graze lazily behind fences. An occasional farm tractor rumbles by. Hay is stacked high in the fields. Rabbits scurry under bushes. Grass is growing tall along the path, and I brush it aside as I walk. I'm a mile outside the little village where I am staying, enjoying my private time with Jesus...

Through the love and power of God I am coming back to the world of missionary ministry, in answer to the prayers of many. I am writing this to thank all of you who love me and have been praying for me with all your hearts. I am excited to tell you that you have not poured yourselves out in vain!

I have been in a battle that has lasted almost two years. In July of 2007 I experienced a nervous breakdown that resulted in a lot of mental and emotional stress. Doctors prescribed medications that only partially helped and had negative side effects. I had a nervous tension that was oppressive and extremely unpleasant. As time went on my memory slipped more and more until I had signs of serious dementia. Heidi was patient and loving, promising to take care of me, but was extremely concerned and beginning to prepare for the worst.

I had a choice between giving in to despair, or inheriting God's promises through faith and patience. There is only up and down, and I chose up. You my friends did not give up on me, but prayers began to rise up to heaven all over the world on my behalf.

I was invited here in Germany a little over a month ago by a beautiful couple we have known for years. They heard about my condition, and were determined to help me through their long experience with medical and natural remedies... They have loved on me and extended themselves to me financially and time-wise in an amazingly unique way. They also run a small hotel, restaurant and "Wellness Center" with saunas, a weight room, massage rooms, alkali scrub tables, all in a beautifully, meticulously built center—mostly the result of voluntary labor. And so I accepted their invitation and have been staying with them in their guest house.

I have gotten a tremendous amount of treatment— they've spared nothing to get my body and me healthy again. This has involved a sophisticated series of injections designed to build up depleted organs, like the adrenal glands (mine were down and out). Then I've had a lot of IV infusions designed to do many things, clean out brain capillaries, wake up my nervous system that gives me sleep and rest, give massive doses of needed vitamins and other things my body was very low on. And then I also got medications of all kinds for various purposes, restoring needed chemicals in the body and brain. It has been an all-out effort on the part of my hosts to do everything possible for me...

All this past month, the staff here have also been praying for me, counseling me and interceding for me intensely. And I've been receiving email from so many of you, telling me of your heart and your prayers for me. The bottom line is that now I am thinking clearly and normally, which is huge. I do not have dementia. The road has been long and difficult, but I am greatly blessed and encouraged. Thank you for not giving up on me, and for persevering with me through everything. I cannot thank you enough! I have a ways to go to settle my nervous condition down, but I am confident in the Lord of victory. Bless you for continuing to pray!

My expenses here have still been considerable, so I want to thank from my heart those of you who are contributing to the mercy fund that was opened on my behalf. The beauty of the body of Christ is great, and I am blessed and moved by you and your sensitivity. Jesus knows what I need, and how to deliver it.

The ministry in Mozambique continues to thrive and grow. The presence of God is strong. Visiting teams are going out to the villages, seeing the blind and deaf healed. Our mission school is in session, and students are in training for a life of mission ministry. The children in our care are worshiping Jesus and praying their hearts out for people and the needs of our work. Churches are being added to our Iris family all the time. Our staff is busy, full of good works and the love of God. We are expanding in many other countries as well.

All this requires a large financial budget, and again we owe you a huge debt of love for supporting us so faithfully, even in a depressed economy. You are making possible our life work, and your continued sensitivity is a sign and a wonder to us. Bless you for fleshing out your spiritual life with concrete financial support. Thank you, thank you! Jesus knows what we need, and you are listening.

That's my news. I look forward to writing you again soon with more encouraging reports on all that Jesus is doing in our lives, and especially in my own life and body. May Jesus be with you in return in every way. May faith and patience be yours in abundance!

Much, much love in Jesus, Rolland

Heidi was just as surprised as everyone else. She couldn't have imagined the drastic changes that had been taking place in Rolland's body and mind in those weeks. She thought the doctors had already tried everything, and she had certainly prayed for Rolland again and again, with no tangible results.

He had clearly improved, but she still had questions. Was he really back? What would he be like in person? She wondered aloud to me, saying he was very sweet and gentle when she spoke with him on the phone. Rolland told her that he was feeling good.

After being a caretaker for the last few years, Heidi would certainly welcome having Rolland back. She found an old wedding photo of the two of them and put it on the kitchen counter to prepare her heart for the return of her husband.

Chapter 22

WELCOME HOME

W HEN ROLLAND RETURNED to Pemba from Germany in the late summer of 2009, Heidi was on the same flight coming back from a monthlong speaking tour around the world. The whole Iris center—all two hundred of the children, the Mozambican staff, the missionaries, and even some of the visitors—met them at the airport. The Iris group filled the entire airport parking lot. The kids had drawn and painted signs for them that said: "We love you, Mama Aida and Papa Rolland" and "Welcome home, Papa Rolland!" One sign had stick figure pictures of Heidi and Rolland looking like Barbie and a soldier. The kids gathered under the trees directly in front of the door where the Bakers would exit, and they sang together, "Welcome home, Mama Aida and Papa."

Heidi exited first, dressed in black with low black heels and black leggings under her black dress. On her arm she carried her Marc Jacobs handbag; gradually she had gotten rid of the poverty mentality when she saw the fruit of it was burnout. The poor didn't want her to be poor; they wanted her to help them out of poverty.

Rolland followed behind her. It had been months since anyone had seen him. Before he left, he was a shell of his former self. Everyone was eager to see Rolland the way he was before he was sick. Heidi had nicknamed him Tigger because of his exuberant joy and the way he jumped up and down when he got excited as he preached. They were all ready to see Tigger back.

Heidi ran to hug the kids. She was thrilled. She made her rounds, hugging each one, including all of the missionaries and visitors. Rolland looked around, greeting those who ran to hug him and welcome him home, but unlike Heidi, who stopped for each person, Rolland kept moving toward the car. He seemed to enjoy the welcome, but he also seemed tired and eager to get home. It would have been overwhelming for anyone. He allowed himself to be driven home by Alberto while Heidi stayed at the airport, greeting everyone.

It took Heidi over an hour to greet everyone. It was like a wedding reception line, except way more chaotic and fun. She flitted easily among the kids, who shouted and competed for her attention. She gave it freely to each one, and then in her heels she climbed up onto the back of the flatbed truck to ride with two hundred of her sons and daughters to the beach, where she kicked off her shoes to race with them in the sand. In the middle of every game and relay, she looked like she was relishing each moment.

Rolland came to the beach after Heidi, where he stood on the sidelines watching the games. Though he appeared to be more of an observer than Heidi, who was in the center of things, the kids warmly welcomed him home. Some of them hugged him, and the ones who knew him well joked with him and felt they had succeeded when he cracked a smile.

Senito, a fourteen-year-old boy from the village whose step-father beat him, strode up to Rolland. "It's good to see you, Papa Rolland," he said in near perfect English. "How are you feeling?"

"Better, much better," Rolland replied, laughing, delighted in the boy's concern for him and surprised at his emotional maturity.

"I am so glad to see you," Senito said.

"It's great to be back," Rolland replied.

He was indeed back. People from all over the world were rejoicing over his healing. They had been following the Bakers' story for years, and when Rolland became sick, they followed his journey even more closely.

People could hardly believe it when, months after returning from Germany, after having been pronounced a dead man by his doctors, Rolland passed his pilot's test and got his license renewed. The health requirements were stringent, and he had passed, proof that his health was restored.

It was almost as if he never had dementia, except that the people who knew and loved him wouldn't easily forget how sick he had been for those two years and how they had almost lost him.

As amazing as Rolland's healing was, the hard times weren't quite over for him and Heidi. A few years later, in February 2012, it was Heidi's turn to fight death.

Heidi had open sores on her arms. She called her doctor in the States, who prescribed antibiotics for multi-resistant staph infection (MRSA). In April it still hadn't gone away, and she was hospitalized in California for ten days and treated intravenously with some of the strongest antibiotics known to man.

Heidi agonized over having to cancel some of her speaking events. She was passionate about the calling on her life to preach the gospel around the world. She had an event in England scheduled for the coming weekend.

It was Thursday morning when the doctor gave her the last IV of antibiotics to treat the MRSA. On Thursday afternoon she got on a flight to England. When she arrived in London on Friday, she collapsed in the hotel room, sleeping the day away, trying to gain the strength to speak to the hundreds of people who would be eagerly waiting for her the next day in the cathedral.

The conference organizer had already been informed she was sick, and he was on standby with a backup plan just in case she couldn't make it.

Heidi called me on the phone, as I was now helping Heidi plan her schedule and travel itineraries. "I think I made a mistake in coming," she said.

"It's not too late to cancel; they have a plan B. You should just rest and regain your strength."

"But I've come all this way. I have to speak now; I'm already here."

Despite my reassurances she pushed through and ministered in the cathedral on Saturday and Sunday morning, and then she flew to northern England to minister on Sunday night and Monday morning. Afterward, the host took her on a tour of the city, wanting to entertain her, not knowing how sick she was. Heidi didn't tell him.

By the time she arrived back in London on Monday evening for a three-day rest, she was very weak. Though she had planned to visit friends, she couldn't leave her hotel room for the entire three days. Scheduled to speak at another conference, she flew into Sweden still very sick, but she wanted to honor her commitments. I met her in Sweden.

Her Norwegian friends were in Sweden for the conference, and because they knew how sick she was, they tried to arrange for someone else to speak on Heidi's behalf so she would have more time to rest, but Heidi wanted to speak. In the two-day conference she spoke three times. By Saturday evening she was so exhausted from severe dehydration that she laid on a mat in the front of the conference meeting room during the worship time. When she began preaching, she was shaky at first and held onto the podium for support, but as she began to get into the message, she appeared stronger—and full of joy. I could hardly tell she was sick.

Afterward, however, she collapsed. All night long she shivered as fever raged in her body, her teeth chattering as sweat soaked the bedsheets.

In the morning we were supposed to meet at eight in the lobby of the hotel to depart for the airport. When she didn't show, I knocked on her hotel room door. She was still in bed, unable to shower or even pack.

"Oh Heidi, I'm so sorry. Why didn't you call me?"

"I didn't want to wake you."

"That's silly. That's why I'm here. What do you want to do? Do you want to cancel the conference in Germany and stay here?"

"I can't stay here…" Her tone was weak but determined. "If you could help me pack, that'd be great," she said.

I gathered the items from the bathroom first, making them fit into her already full bags. She traveled so often she had mastered fitting what she needed into two small bags.

We left for the airport twenty minutes late, and she laid down in the backseat of the van. I carried her bags through the airport while she struggled to appear healthy so the airline would permit her on the plane. Walking was a challenge, so we had to go slowly.

We both had flights to Amsterdam, and then she was supposed to go on to Germany and I was taking a train to the south of Holland to meet my husband; in two days we were all flying back to Mozambique. On the short flight she slept, and I thought about what to do. Surely she couldn't speak tonight at a conference in Germany.

When we arrived in Amsterdam, Heidi said she couldn't go any further, not even on the train to the tropical disease hospital in Antwerp. She told me to go and that she would call me later. I told her that I wouldn't leave until she was feeling better. We would stay in Amsterdam so she could rest. She agreed that we should call the event organizer and cancel; though they were sorely disappointed, they said they would be praying for Heidi.

She was exhausted from the pace of the conference in Sweden, and she went to take a nap while I raided the pharmacy in the airport, spending close to two hundred euros on rehydration packets, probiotics, and other vitamins and medicines the pharmacist recommended.

When I returned, Heidi was on the phone with her longtime pastor friend from California. She could barely raise her voice to a whisper, and he could tell that she was very sick. Otherwise she would not have called. Heidi rarely asked for help.

"You must go to the clinic in Germany where Rolland was treated," he told her.

"There are medical doctors there, right?" Heidi asked.

"Oh yes, oh yes, they have doctors."

Heidi couldn't even keep liquid in her system, but the rehydration packets helped her regain some fluids, and after sleeping all day and night, she felt a bit stronger the next morning, and I was able to help her get to the clinic in Germany. Unfortunately the natural clinic did not have medical doctors there as she had been told, so Heidi's ten-day stay passed without the root issues of MRSA and C. diff, which she had also contracted, being treated with antibiotics or traditional medicine. The infections were serious, and no one knew what the MRSA was doing; the worst-case scenario was that it would travel to her bloodstream.

Heidi decided she should fly to South Africa for treatment, but once we were on the plane to South Africa, Heidi said, "I might just want to go straight back to Pemba. I'm not sure I want to stop in South Africa."

"Why don't you think about it and see how you feel after the flight?" I suggested gently, terrified that Heidi would return to Pemba, the bush town with no medical care.

When we arrived in Johannesburg, she said, "I just want to go home." Though I thought it unwise because of the lack of medical care available in Pemba, she just wanted to go home, and I knew it wouldn't work to try to convince her otherwise. We headed to the airline ticket counter and bought two tickets to Pemba. On the plane we went over last-minute administrative details so she could rest when she got home.

When Heidi and I arrived in Pemba, she called together her closest friends and coworkers. There were seven or eight of us crowded into her room while she lay in the center of the bed. One of her friends played the keyboard and sang worship choruses so Heidi could relax and wouldn't have to talk. Then near the end of the evening, one of Heidi's former assistants who was back for a visit asked about the film team she had brought with her, and Heidi started planning her weekly schedule as if it were any other normal week. It was hardly modified from her typical heavy routine. She wanted to show the film crew as much as possible since they had come all the way from the States to see her in action in Mozambique.

The Iris doctor on staff had just finished telling me that Heidi absolutely needed to be on bed rest in order to heal. The medicine she was being given was so strong that her immune system needed all the rest possible. But when I went back into the room, Heidi was already making lists of everything she had to do, and everyone was listening intently to her as usual and nodding in agreement to her overly ambitious itinerary.

"Heidi! You can't do that. The doctor just told me how serious this is! He said you absolutely need to be on bed rest or you're risking everything, You've already been dealing with this for months, and you haven't been able to get better because you haven't slowed down. Please rest. You're making yourself sick!"

The others looked at me in surprise because none of them knew how serious Heidi's illness was.

Heidi laughed weakly and looked away as if to say she knew I was right. She wasn't able to even vocalize to the others how sick she was, and when she heard me say it out loud, she acquiesced a bit.

"Well, I can't cancel everything, but I can limit it. I can cut out a few things and just have all my meetings at home from bed."

A few minutes later she went out to talk to the doctor. He told her how sick she was and that she needed to rest, but he wasn't as emphatic with her as he had been with me because she was his leader.

"Tell her what you told me! Tell her how you said it is dangerous if she's not on bed rest!"

"It really is, Heidi," he said as if talking to a child now, but he didn't elaborate. I could tell Heidi wasn't taking him seriously, and it scared me.

In the kitchen I approached her again. "You're scaring me, Heidi. Why are you doing this? Can't you just rest for a week? Then you'll feel so much better. If you keep going like this, it will take much longer to heal, and you've already been sick for so long!"

Her eyes were smiling at me. I could tell that she appreciated my concern, because I cared about her, but at the same time she seemed to be saying, "My work is more important than my good health."

I put my arm around her waist. "It's so hard to watch someone I love hurt herself."

"I'll be fine," she said, her eyes still smiling.

Heidi tried to take the medical staff's advice to rest by

working only a regular eight-hour day instead of the usual twelve to fourteen hours. Around five in the afternoon, Heidi would go home and lie down on her bed while the Iris medical staff hooked her up to an IV of antibiotics and vitamins. Then she started all over again the next day, refusing to rest until she spent every last bit of energy she had.

While connected to the IV drip, Heidi took calls from all over the world. There was a donor organization in Virginia that wanted to give her funds to build ten thousand more church buildings, another contact was calling her about returning to Boston to speak at the meeting he was arranging for Ivy League college students, and she spent time on the phone making plans for the university she wanted to build in Pemba. A few months earlier she had spoken at a US university, and the university president told Heidi they would help her with the Mozambican university any way they could.

Iris had transitioned from a mom-and-pop ministry to a medium-sized organization, and Heidi and Rolland were both working at breakneck speed. There were so many things happening at once because there was just so much need.

The biggest struggle was figuring out how to maintain freedom while still functioning like an organization. The Bakers were seeking God for the right amount of structure. Rolland was especially passionate about not creating structures that would limit the Holy Spirit. They were learning and adapting along the way as their organization grew very quickly. As everyone was walking out this transition together, sometimes communication lines were crossed, the work was messy, or multiple people were asked to perform the same task, but to them these results were better than control or over-management.

When Heidi's body finally healed of the MRSA, many months later during the fall of 2012, she began traveling

again, her talks centering around legacy and empowering
the next generation, and she invited twenty-five of her spiritual sons and daughters to spend three days with her and
Rolland. The three-day gathering was a welcomed time of
slowing down. To the Bakers twenty-five people seemed like
a small, intimate group.

Because Heidi was now focusing on legacy, she asked each
of us to share what we were currently working toward. She
was usually the one asked to speak, but during these days, she
really wanted to listen. It was about the next generation now,
and she really wanted them to feel her support and know that
she was cheering them on because sometimes that was what
sons and daughters needed most.

A few years after his healing, Rolland completed a PhD program, wrote his dissertation, and finally received his doctorate,
ultimate proof that his brain was just fine.

Rolland dedicated his dissertation to Heidi and his biological children, and wrote in the acknowledgments: "First of all,
I must acknowledge my wife Heidi for her unswerving confidence that Jesus wanted me to finish this degree program,
and her never-ending faith that it would happen in spite of
the intensity, pressures and challenges of our nonstop ministry in Africa and around the world. Her affectionate love
and support, and even stubborn insistence, was crucial to me.
The core values of Iris have originated as much through her as
through me, and in many ways this is 'our' project. For many
years her giftings and encounters with God have given her
the faith, love, initiative, courage and endurance to model our
core values daily for the world to see. Iris Global would not
exist without her, and I would not be writing this document
without my history with her."[1]

At Rolland's graduation ceremony, United Theological Seminary invited Heidi to give the commencement speech. "If you don't believe in miracles, just look at Rolland. The doctors said he had terminal dementia and would forget how to swallow. He's a walking miracle," she said. Then she cheered.

The president of the seminary asked Heidi to join them in hooding Rolland. Heidi stood in front of her husband, her eyes shining with pride and congratulations, as he received the highest academic distinction. She helped lower the hood, then cupped her hands lovingly under his chin and hugged him tightly around his neck.

AFTERWORD

HEIDI'S VISION FOR Iris is to care for a million children in her lifetime. With so many people looking to her as their mentor and spiritual mother, she may be closer than she realizes.

After an Iris missionary from the UK spent time in Mozambique being trained by Heidi and Rolland, she had a vision of abandoned babies in garbage dumps. When she learned that this frequently happened in Madagascar, she knew she had to go. She had few resources when she arrived in Madagascar, but through the generous support of friends and family she was able to buy a house and now cares for many abandoned toddlers and babies. Though she was single at the time, she didn't let that stop her from adopting and becoming a mom to so many.

Some of Heidi's adopted sons and daughters whom she raised were also going out to other countries. Some are missionaries in other nations; others have gone to the United States to visit and sometimes speak in churches where Heidi has contacts. The Bakers' biological and spiritual children are flourishing and are huge additions to the organization.

When I left Mozambique, Heidi and Rolland were both healthy, though they were still trying to learn to balance work and rest. The future looked bright as additional Iris programs continued to spring up all over the world that would equip more and more people to change the world through service and love, even when it meant sacrifice.

Did Heidi know what lay ahead when she was sixteen years old and heard God say she would be a missionary—the joy unspeakable but also the sorrow, the pain of self-sacrifice, flames licking up everything around her? She would drink from the cup of joy and suffering, but she would use the pain and allow it to drive her back to solitude, to love, to something altogether foreign and separate from the scorched desert places she often found herself in.

God asked her for everything and she gave it all, and in return she received living water, joy, new life that came every time she gave hers away.

From Laguna Beach to Switzerland to central Mississippi to Mexico City to Indonesia to the Philippines to Hong Kong to London to Mozambique, Heidi would remain the girl who discovered how to love others from the inside—who would love with arms wide open. Mama Aida.

To thousands of children she has given a love that feels like coming home, no matter that she had to set herself on fire in order to do so. Like Thomas Merton, an Oxford intellectual who gave up his privilege and the world's pleasures to adopt the austere lifestyle of a monk, Heidi Baker learned to know "the Christ of the burnt men."[1]

NOTES

INTRODUCTION
1. John 15:13.

CHAPTER 5—FIRST LOVE
1. Luke 14:26–27.

CHAPTER 10—MAPUTO

1. Malyn Newitt, *A History of Mozambique* (Braamfontein, Johannesburg, South Africa: Wits University Press, 1995).
2. Kevin Shillington, *A History of Africa* (Basingstoke, United Kingdom: Palgrave Macmillan, 2005).
3. Ibid.
4. Stephanie Schwartz, *Youth and Post-Conflict Reconstruction: Agents of Change* (Washington, DC: United States Institute of Peace Press, 2010).

CHAPTER 15—EXPANSION

1. Sandra Block, "Insurance Losses Minimal From Tsunami," *USA Today*, December 28, 2004, accessed December 8, 2015, http://usatoday30.usatoday.com/money/world/2004-12-28-insure-usat_x.htm.

CHAPTER 17—THE IRIS FAMILY
1. In communication with the author, March 2006.

CHAPTER 18—WOMEN WERE MADE IN GOD'S IMAGE TOO

1. "Mozambique," CIA World Factbook, accessed December 8, 2015, https://www.cia.gov/library/publications/the-world-factbook/geos/mz.html.
2. Constantina Michalos, "'You Shall Hear the Nightingale Sing on as if in Pain': The Philomena Myth as Metaphor of Transformation and Resistance in the Works of Susan Glaspell and Alice Walker" (doctoral thesis, Rice University, 1996).

CHAPTER 20—IN NEED OF A MIRACLE

1. Candy Brown, "Study of the Therapeutic Effects of Proximal Intercessory Prayer (STEPP) on Auditory and Visual Impairments in Rural Mozambique," *Southern Medical Journal*, September 2010.

CHAPTER 21—GERMANY

1. Used with permission.

CHAPTER 22—WELCOME HOME

1. Rolland Baker, "Toward a Biblical 'Strategy' of Mission: The Effects of the Five Christian 'Core Values' of Iris Global" (PhD dissertation, United Theological Seminary, 2013).

AFTERWORD

1. Thomas Merton, *The Seven Storey Mountain* (New York: Harcourt, Inc., 1998).

CONNECT WITH US!

CHARISMA HOUSE

(Spiritual Growth)

f Facebook.com/CharismaHouse

t @CharismaHouse

O Instagram.com/CharismaHouseBooks

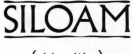

(Health)

P Pinterest.com/CharismaHouse

REALMS

(Fiction)

f Facebook.com/RealmsFiction